2   J.   020330

PEOPLES ON THE MOVE

The Transatlantic Slave Trade

AM I NOT A MAN AND A BROTHER.

David Killingray

B.T. Batsford Ltd, London

Contents

© David Killingray 1987

First published 1987

Typeset by Tek-Art Ltd, Kent
and printed in Great Britain by
R J Acford Ltd,
Chichester, Sussex
for the publishers
B.T. Batsford Ltd
4 Fitzhardinge Street
London W1H 0AH

ISBN 0 7134 5469 5

Frontispiece
*An eighteenth-century engraving of the seal of the
Committee for the Abolition of the Slave Trade
(Wilberforce Museum, Hull)*

Foreword

Throughout history people have been on the move from one place to another. In this way a large part of the world has become inhabited. For most of human history people moved in small groups, searching for new lands where they could live free from enemies and hunger.

The greatest migration, or movement, of people occurred between 1820 and 1930 and was made possible by the development of the railway and the steam ship. During that period millions of people made the long journey from Europe to America, but also to Australia and New Zealand, and from European Russia eastwards into Siberia. Smaller movements of people also took place in Asia, with Chinese moving into the lands and islands of Southeast Asia and Japanese out into the Pacific and to America.

Most people moved as a result of what can crudely be described as a mixture of "push" and "pull" factors. They were "pushed" out of their homes by poor living conditions, shortage of land, or lack of religious and political freedoms, and "pulled" or attracted to new lands and countries by the hope of a better way of life and new opportunities. For some people migration was largely involuntary: either they did not want to move or they had very little choice. Between 1520 and 1870 millions of Africans were forcibly taken across the Atlantic to America as slaves, and today there are millions of refugees in the world who have been compelled to leave their homes because of war, famine and disease.

Migration mixes people together, not only people from different parts of the same country but also peoples of different languages and cultures. Countries such as the United States and Brazil have been created by people from vastly different backgrounds. And if we look closely at the history of Britain we will see that our language and culture have been shaped by migrants coming to these islands during the last thousand years or more. Migration from Europe to the new lands after 1700 led to the spread of languages (English and Spanish to the Americas, for example), the development of new accents and new cultures, or ways of life.

The aim of this series of books is to look at different examples of "peoples on the move" – why did they leave their original homes? How did they travel? What did they take with them? What did they find in the new lands? How did they settle down? What were relations like between "natives" and newcomers? And what was the impact of new economic systems on the land?

If you have had the experience of moving home, perhaps from one country to another, or even from one place to another *within* a country, then you may be able to share the feelings of people who migrated in the past. If you have never moved home then perhaps these books will help you to understand the reasons why people move, and why in the world today there are, for example, people of European origin living in America and South Africa, and people of African and Asian origin living also in America and in Britain.

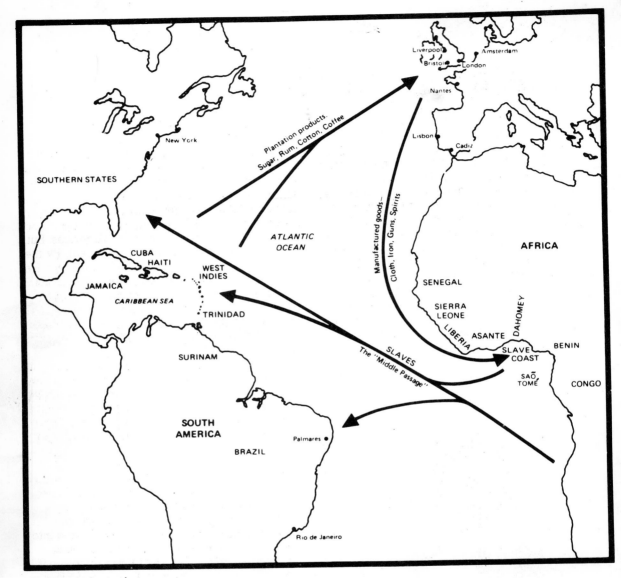

The triangular trade.

1 The Adventurous Life of Olaudah Equiano

An African boy aged 11, and his small sister, played happily in the yard of the walled compound which surrounded their family home. Their parents were out in the fields working. Suddenly a man and woman climbed over the wall, seized both children, held their mouths to stifle their cries for help, and carried them off into the surrounding forest. When they had gone a good distance from the village the kidnappers tied the hands of the children behind their backs and forced them to walk ahead of them. Olaudah Equiano and his sister had become slaves.

After several days' travelling Olaudah's sister was sold and he never saw her again. It was, he remembered many years later, "a day of greater sorrow than I had yet experienced". Shortly afterwards he, too, was sold – to an African blacksmith who needed a child to work the bellows of his furnace.

Portrait of Olaudah Equiano, 1789. Dressed as a gentleman, with a powdered wig, Equiano holds in his hand a Bible open at Acts, Chapter 4, Verse 12 to emphasize his Christian faith.

This was the start of the adventurous life of Olaudah Equiano, an Igbo boy from the area that is now part of south-eastern Nigeria. His experiences were similar to those of many hundreds of thousands of Africans in the years between 1520 and 1860 who were enslaved in Africa and then sold to European traders and shipped across the Atlantic to the Americas. But, in many ways, Equiano was exceptional. By the time that he was 21 he was no longer a slave. He was able to buy his freedom, to settle in Britain, where he married an English woman, and also to write an autobiography which he called *The Interesting Narrative of the Life of Olaudah Equiano, or Gustavus Vassa, The African*, published in 1789.

Equiano made an unsuccessful attempt to escape from his African master, who eventually sold him. After several more owners the young slave was eventually brought to the coast. It was a dramatic moment for Equiano, who never before had seen the sea, ships, or Europeans. Many years later he wrote:

The first object which saluted my eyes when I arrived on the coast was the sea, and a slave ship which was then riding at anchor and waiting for its cargo. These filled me with astonishment, which was soon converted into terror when I was carried on board. I was immediately handled and tossed up to see if I were sound by some of the crew, and I was now persuaded that I had gotten into a world of bad spirits and that they were going to kill me. Their complexions too differing so much from ours, their long hair and the language they spoke (which was very different from any I had ever heard) united to confirm me in this belief.

Lined up with other men, women and children, many of them chained together to prevent escape, Equiano was taken aboard the European slaver. Desperately frightened and harshly

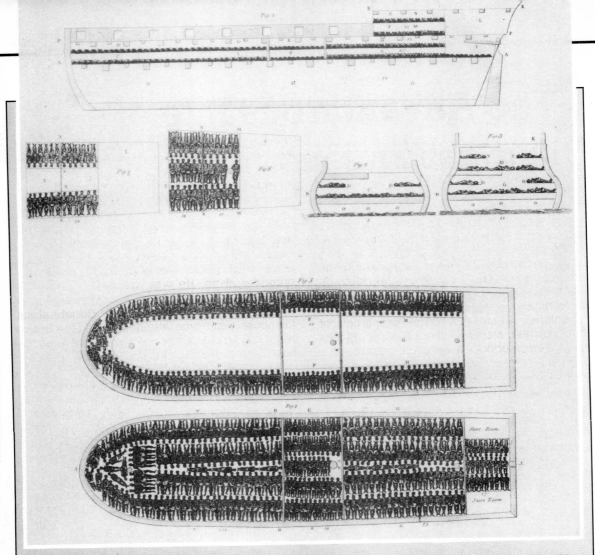

Plan of the British slaver Brookes.

Thomas Clarkson as a young man wrote a prize-winning essay at Cambridge entitled "Is it Right to Make Slaves of Others Against Their Will?". He became an active opponent of the slave trade. In Bristol he collected first-hand information from sailors and merchants about the conditions of both slaves and the seamen on slaving ships. In his *The History of the Rise, Progress, and Accomplishment of the Abolition of the African Slave Trade by the British Parliament*, published in 1808, Clarkson described the slaver *Brookes* as having a lower deck length of 100 feet, a breadth of 25 feet 4 inches, and the height between decks as being 5 feet.

treated, the slaves were often unsure of what was happening or where they were going. The human cargo was forced below decks and chained in the hold while the ship got underway. The bewildering and terrifying experience of being crammed into the cramped and claustrophobic hold of the slave ship remained printed on Equiano's mind.

The stench of the hold was intolerably loathsome. The closeness of the place and heat of the climate, added to the number in the ship, which was so crowded that each had scarcely room to turn himself, almost suffocated us. The air became unfit to breathe and many of the slaves fell sick and died. Our wretched situation was aggravated by the heavy chains on our legs, the filth of the necessary tubs, and the shrieks of women and the groans of the dying.

After many weeks at sea, during which time a good number of the slaves died from disease and despair, the ship reached the Caribbean island of Barbados. The slaves were landed and most sold by auction.

Slaves were found throughout all the European colonies in the Americas. Nearly all were Black, and their colour was usually a badge of their inferiority and enslavement. They formed the major part of the labour force, working on plantations, in mines, small factories and workshops, in houses, as seamen, craftsmen, and as personal servants. A large proportion of Whites owned slaves. Although some Blacks gained their freedom, slaves could generally be bought and sold at will, just like cattle. Very few

laws protected them against the cruel treatment that some owners inflicted on them. Many of the American colonial economies were slave economies. Their great wealth was based on profits gained from the work of Black slaves who grew crops such as sugar, tobacco, and cotton, which were then exported to European markets.

Equiano was not sold in Barbados but with a few other slaves was shipped to Virginia, one of the British colonies in North America. There his first European owner kept a plantation. Large numbers of slaves were employed in the tobacco fields but Equiano was kept in the house as a domestic slave. He was dressed in European clothes and given the new name of Jacob. His job was to wait on his mistress and do odd-jobs about the house. Some time later he was sold to a British naval officer and renamed Gustavus Vassa. By now Equiano had learnt some English. His new owner took his young slave to England and

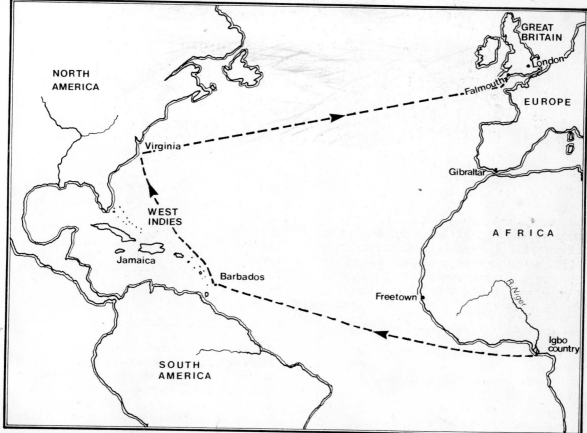

Map to show the travels of Olaudah Equiano in the eighteenth century.

Equiano records his surprise on arriving at Falmouth in the winter of 1757 and seeing the houses and streets covered with snow.

For four years Equiano accompanied his master on board various warships and he served as a "powder monkey", carrying gunpowder to the cannon, at a great naval battle against the French off Gibraltar. During this time Equiano learned to read and write and he also became a Christian, being baptised in St Margaret's Church, Westminster, in London. Equiano now thought that because he had worked loyally and lived in Britain for several years he had earned his freedom. But his master, who had generally been kind to him, suddenly became very unpleasant and sold Equiano to a ship bound for the Caribbean. Back in the West Indian colonies Equiano was bought by a Quaker trader and ship-owner. He was employed as a seaman on boats plying between the islands and to the North American ports. The Quaker was a kindly owner and in 1767, just over ten years after his capture in West Africa, Equiano was able to buy his freedom with money he had earned in trading.

This was not the end of his adventures – he was shipwrecked, served with a Royal Navy expedition searching for the north-west passage through the Arctic seas and was again a seaman in the Caribbean – but finally he settled in Britain.

In the 1780s and 1790s Equiano became active in the anti-slave trade movement and particularly in the scheme to settle poor Blacks from Britain in West Africa. This led to the establishment of the colony of Freetown in 1787, a town that is now the capital city of Sierra Leone. Although Equiano hoped also to return to West Africa he never achieved his ambition. He died in Britain, probably in 1801.

Despite his tragic childhood Equiano was much more fortunate than millions of other slaves

"The Death of Nelson", engraving by C.W. Sharpe. Notice the Black sailor.

torn from Africa and shipped to the Americas. Few gained their freedom; their lives were often nasty, brutish and short. When Equiano arrived in Britain as a boy there were probably 15-20,000 Black people in the country and many more living in other European states such as Portugal, Spain, France, and Holland. Since the start of the European slave trade with Africa in the fifteenth century Blacks had settled in Europe as slaves, servants and seamen. Their numbers increased as the slave trade grew. Africans were also taken by Arab and African slave traders across the Sahara and the Red Sea to North Africa, Arabia, Iran and India. Today there are millions of people of African origin who live outside Africa and who are the result of that great Black diaspora, or forced scattering of people. This book looks at this movement of Black people from Africa, mainly to the Americas, brought about by the slave trade.

2 West Africa before 1500

Africa is a vast continent containing many types of terrain and varieties of vegetation. There are huge deserts, such as the rocky wastes of the Sahara, mountains tipped with snow and cut by glaciers which stand astride the Equator, and the tropical rain forests of the West African coast and the Zaïre (Congo) river basin. But a large part of sub-Saharan Africa is rolling savanna grassland, much of it in eastern, central and southern Africa being relatively cool uplands. West and equatorial Africa, the areas most affected by the transatlantic slave trade, have a hot, tropical climate and heavy seasonal rainfall.

The term "African" is often used as if the inhabitants of the continent belonged to a single identifiable group. Africans are diverse in language and appearance. For example, the Asante from modern Ghana, who speak Twi, have a very different culture from the Yoruba, who live only 500 kilometres to the east in what are now the republics of Benin and Nigeria, or from the Fulani-speaking cattle herders of the semi-arid Sahelian region 1000 kilometres to the north.

Over the past 2000 years Africa has been a continent of human movement. Small groups of people have moved into thinly populated lands and established new farming settlements, villages, and towns. One of the most important continuous movements was the slow spread of people from western Africa into central and southern Africa. About 2000 years ago people who spoke the original Bantu language (known as Proto-Bantu) moved from the Cameroons into the savanna lands of central Africa before slowly dispersing throughout southern and eastern Africa. These movements continued well into the nineteenth century and, today, Bantu languages are spoken by most people in the continent south of the Equator. Although these languages have a common origin (like English, Dutch and German) they are not mutually intelligible. Bantu-speaking peoples carried with them into the savanna lands a knowledge of iron-working. Their iron tools and weapons helped them to clear the land for

farming and also to defeat opponents who stood in their way.

Although most people in Africa today live in villages and work in agriculture Africa has a long history of settlement in towns. The growth of towns has often been closely associated with trade. In the grasslands of West Africa towns developed as cultural and trading centres. The great empires of the western Sudan – Ghana, Mali, and Songhai – owed their wealth and power

The Trade of Hausaland
Some of our knowledge about early Africa comes from archaeological evidence. But there are also many written sources, especially for certain areas of North Africa and the Sudanic region stretching from the Red Sea to the Atlantic Ocean. The word "sudan" comes from the Arabic *Bilad al-Sudan*, "the Land of the Blacks". One of the earliest records of the Hausa trading states of what is now northern Nigeria is *The Kano Chronicle*, which was written in Arabic. This extract describes the trade of the Hausa states during the reign of Yakubu *c*. 1452-63:

... In Yakubu's time the Fulani came to Hausaland from Mali, bringing with them books on Divinity and Etymology. Formerly our doctors had, in addition to the Qur'an, only the books of the Law and the Traditions [*Hadith*]. The Fulani passed by and went to Bornu leaving a few men in Hausaland, together with some slaves and people who were tired of journeying. At this time too the Absbenawa [traders from Sahara] came to Gobir, and salt became common in Hausaland. In the following year merchants from Gwanja [Gonja in northern Ghana] began coming to Katsina .... There was no war in Hausaland in Yakubu's time.
(H.R. Palmer, ed., *The Kano Chronicle*, included in *Sudanese Memoirs*, Vol. III, 1928, p. 111)

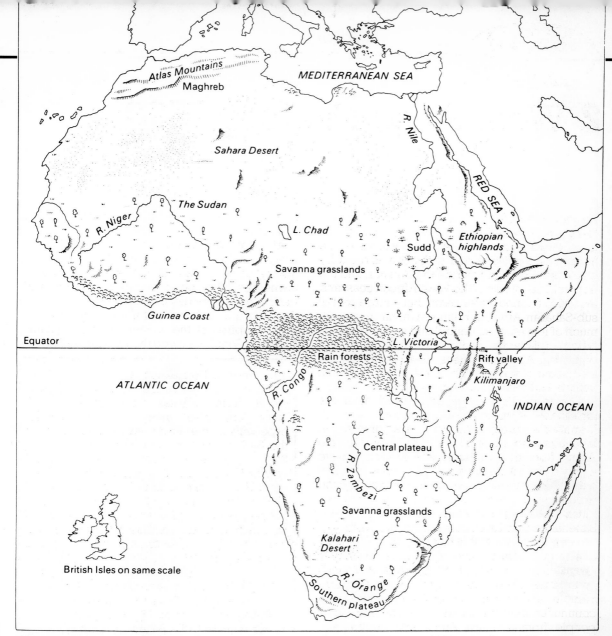

African regions and barriers.

Labels on map: Atlas Mountains, Maghreb, MEDITERRANEAN SEA, R. Nile, Sahara Desert, RED SEA, The Sudan, R. Niger, L. Chad, Sudd, Ethiopian highlands, Savanna grasslands, Guinea Coast, Equator, L. Victoria, Rain forests, Rift valley, ATLANTIC OCEAN, R. Congo, Kilimanjaro, INDIAN OCEAN, Central plateau, R. Zambezi, Savanna grasslands, Kalahari Desert, British Isles on same scale, R. Orange, Southern plateau

to the trans-Saharan trade which focused on large cities such as Gao, Mopti, Timbuktu, and Jenne. By the early sixteenth century, when Europeans were beginning to trade with the coast of West Africa, some of the most powerful cities were in the area that is now northern Nigeria. For example, by 1500 Kano was an important commercial centre, linking the trade routes across the Sahara with the trading systems that stretched south into the forest states. Within the extensive high mud walls of the city were all manner of trades and crafts involving leather, wood, cloth, and various metals. Food was also grown within and outside the city limits, and Kano was a bustling market for a wide range of agricultural goods which were also used in various industrial processes. Regular caravans of camels and horses, laden with salt, ivory, cloth, and accompanied by slaves, left the city for the long journey to the markets of North Africa. Camels and horses had been introduced into North Africa from Asia around A.D. 400. Their use on the lengthy routes across the parched Sahara lands revolutionized the desert-side economy of West Africa; a larger volume of goods could be carried to and from the trading centres of the

11

The Walled City of Kano

This illustration of the Hausa city of Kano was drawn in the nineteenth century by Heinrich Barth, a European traveller. Kano then had a population of around 30,000 people and was surrounded by a high mud wall over 15 miles in length, which had 14 gates. For several centuries Kano had been a great trading and manufacturing centre. The major industry was weaving and dyeing cotton cloth, which was then exported throughout the region. A large part of Kano's trade was with the markets of North Africa. Camel caravans regularly crossed the Sahara Desert carrying export goods such as salt, leather goods, and slaves, and bringing in return calicoes, silks, and various metal products from the countries of the Mediterranean.

western Sudan and North Africa.

There were also towns in the forest lands nearer to the West African coast. These were centres of political power as well as places for trade and craft work. During the period of the transatlantic slave trade many of these towns grew in influence as the capitals of powerful forest kingdoms.

The trade routes across the Sahara also brought a new and important influence to West Africa – the religion of Islam. Islam, which had originated in Arabia, spread with great rapidity across North Africa during the eighth century A.D. Very gradually, the faith crossed the Sahara by the trade routes and was accepted, usually in an adapted form, by some of the desert-side states. With Islam came many new and influential ideas from Arab North Africa and western Asia: the Arabic script and literacy, ideas about government, law, and architecture. Such ideas and skills helped Islam spread and radically changed the political and social system of many of the states in the western Sudanic region.

Craftsmen and Traders on the River Gambia

Richard Jobson, an English seaman, wrote one of the first accounts in English about the people of the River Gambia region in West Africa. His book, *The Golden Trade*, was published in London in 1623:

There are among the Mandingo three principall Trades, the Smith which of Iron brought to them (for else they have none) makes the Swords, Assegay heads, Darts and Arrow heads barbed; and instruments of Husbandry, without which they could not live. Hee hath his Bellowes, small Anvill, and Cole or a red wood, which alone will give the true heat to our Iron. . . . The next Trade is the Sepatero, or Gregorie maker, made artificially in all shapes, round and square and triangle. . . . They also make Bridles and Saddles, of which I have seene some very neat, hardly to be bettered heere; whereby it seemes they have skill to dress and dye their Deeres skins and Goats skins. A third Profession is of those which temper the Earth for their wals and pots in which they boyle meats, using for other services the gourd. . . . But the generall Trade . . . is Husbandry . . .; They make furrowes as decently as we doe, but with handie labour, having a short sticke about a yard long, on the end of which is a broad Iron which is used for cutting the grounde.

3 Early Contacts between Europe and Africa

The great lake of the Mediterranean linked southern Europe with North Africa. In ancient times the Greeks had colonies on the North African coasts of Egypt and Libya. The Romans conquered a large area of North Africa and those provinces became an important granary, providing food for much of the Empire. Black slaves from the Nile valley and other parts of North Africa were to be found in the homes, plantations and mines of the Greek and Roman slave economies.

After the Arab conquest of North Africa, sea-borne trade across the Mediterranean continued. European merchants traded in all sorts of goods, especially gold brought across the Sahara from the western Sudan, and Black slaves. Slavery was common throughout medieval Europe, particularly in the Mediterranean countries. Slaves came not only from Africa but also from the Black Sea ports and the trading centres in western Asia. But Christian Europe and the Muslim states of North Africa and the eastern Mediterranean were constantly at war with one another. By the fourteenth and fifteenth centuries the Portuguese and Spanish were slowly pushing the Muslim conquerors out of their countries and seizing small possessions in North Africa.

The Islamic states of the southern and eastern shores of the Mediterranean were political and commercial rivals of the Portuguese. They stood in the way of the expanding trade demands of Europe. The Portuguese wanted to have direct access to the gold of West Africa and the spice and other trade goods of Asia. If a sea route could be found around the vast and unknown coast of the African continent it might be possible to open that direct route to the "Far East". Such a route would also bring the Portuguese behind their Muslim opponents and give them a political advantage.

The Portuguese had a long experience of using sailing ships on the dangerous seas of the Atlantic. New types of ship and sail had been developed, and gradually sailors pushed further down the uncharted coast of north-western Africa. By the end of the fourteenth century the Portuguese had reached the Canary Islands. One hundred years later Portuguese sailors arrived off the coast of modern Ghana. There, in 1482, the Portuguese built a solid stone fort named São Jorge de Mina, or Elmina ("the mine"), because it was close to the gold fields in the forest region. A few years later the Portuguese explorer Vasco da Gama rounded the southern tip of Africa, crossed the Indian Ocean, and opened a direct sea route to India and the East.

Among the earliest cargoes taken by Portuguese traders from West Africa were slaves. They were bought from African kings and merchants and transported by ship to the markets of southern Portugal. By the end of the fifteenth century, only a few years after America

Slavery existed throughout much of Europe from Ancient times. In the Mediterranean countries slaves of African origin were very common. This painting by Andrea Mantegna is of an African slave in medieval Italy.

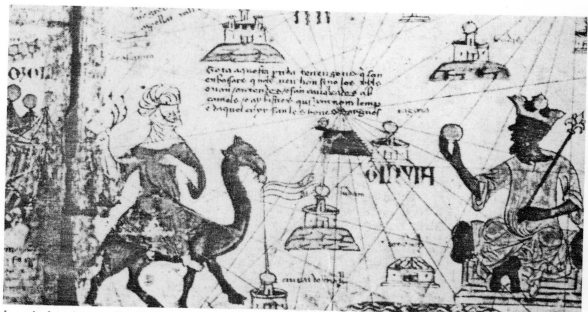

Long before they explored the coast of West Africa, Europeans heard from Arabs about the kingdoms of the western Sudanic region. On the Catalan Map, drawn in Spain in 1375, the Emperor of the state of Mali, Mansu Musa, is shown seated on his throne. Towns and camel caravans are also shown.

had been "discovered" by Columbus, the most southerly province of Portugal, the Algarve, where today many British tourists take their holidays, had a population which was predominantly Black.

The main interest of the Europeans was in the rich trade of Asia, in the silks and spices which could be bought in the markets of India and the East Indian islands. By contrast, Africa had little to offer. West Africa had only a limited range of goods demanded by Europeans and markets that were very much on the periphery of the world trading system. Also, the coast of West Africa had few natural harbours or suitable rivers where ships could lie at anchor. The climate was hot and diseases such as malaria, which people did not know how to prevent, killed or weakened many of the Europeans who went there. Nevertheless, Africa did produce some trade goods for European merchants. Besides gold West Africa also provided ivory, spices (or "grains") like Malaguetta pepper, and, increasingly, slaves. Stretches of the West African coast came to be known after these principal trade goods – the Gold Coast, Ivory Coast, Grain Coast, and the Slave Coast.

The Portuguese imported slaves from West Africa into southern Europe but they also found a use for them on plantations developed in some of the Atlantic islands, such as the Azores and Madeira. On the small island of São Tomé, near to the coast of equatorial Africa and within the Gulf of Biafra, the Portuguese established sugar plantations. Slaves were brought to the island from the kingdom of Kongo and set to work to grow and cut sugar cane for the markets of Europe. Slave imports into São Tomé continued until the 1580s, when a series of major slave revolts destroyed many of the plantations and caused many of the Portuguese settlers to abandon the island.

The Portuguese attempted to plant Christianity in the West African kingdoms of Benin and Kongo. King Nzinga Mvemba of Kongo welcomed the new ideas but greedy Portuguese traders and slavers exploited their position in the kingdom. When Nzinga attempted to stop them from taking slaves from his state he met bitter opposition and attempts were made on his life. But he did succeed in persuading the Portuguese to move their slaving activities southwards out of his kingdom. Christianity only put down very

European trading companies built forts along various stretches of the coast of West Africa. On the Gold Coast there were more than 30 forts. Some were solid stone buildings, like this English fort at Anomabo, with high walls defended with cannon, garrisoned with soldiers and dominating the nearby countryside. Others were little better than weakly defended warehouses in which merchants stored goods to await the arrival of cargo ships.

> Sir, many of our people, keenly desirous of the wares and things of your kingdoms, which are brought here by your many people, and in order to satisfy their greed, seize many of our free people; and very often it happens that they kidnap even noblemen and the sons of noblemen, and our relatives, and take them to be sold to the white men who are in our kingdoms. . . . And to avoid such a great evil we passed a law so that any white man living in our Kingdoms and wanting to purchase goods in any way should first inform three of our noblemen and officials of our court . . . who should investigate if the mentioned goods are captives or free men.
>
> (Letter of protest by Nzinga Mvemba, the Christian *manikongo* [king] of Kongo [1506-43] to the King of Portugal about the effects of the slave trade on his people)

shallow roots in West African states. Priests and teachers were too few in number, although vestiges of Christianity survived in Kongo until as late as the 1650s.

Other European merchants followed the Portuguese to West Africa. They also built trading forts, particularly along stretches of the Gold and Slave Coasts. Dutch, French, English, German and Danish traders all hoped to secure part of the trade of the West African coast.

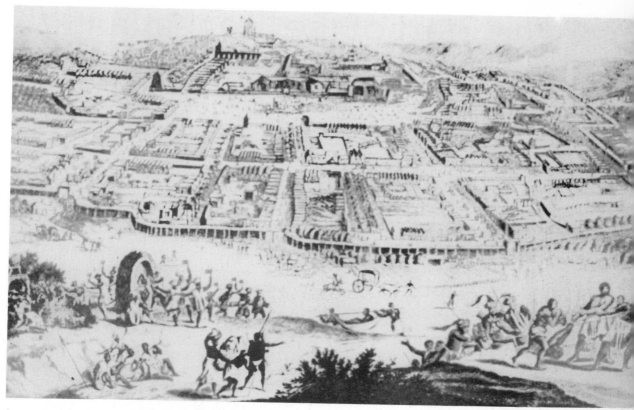

Loango was one of the main cities of the Kingdom of Kongo. The palace of the manikongo (king) is on the top of the hill. A wall surrounds the royal area. In the foreground criminals are being taken away, possibly as slaves.

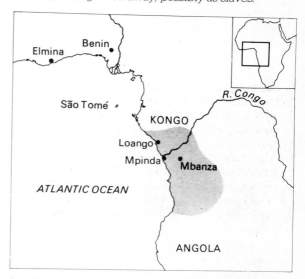

São Tomé and the Kingdom of Kongo 1483-1665.

4 The Start of the Transatlantic Slave Trade

As we have seen, well before Europeans discovered, or rediscovered, America slaves were being brought from West Africa to Portugal and Spain and were also being used on the plantations created on the Atlantic islands. In 1492 Columbus reached the Caribbean and named the islands that he found the "West Indies" – he believed them to be part of India. Columbus claimed the "New World" for the Spanish Crown, but the Spanish Pope decided that Portugal should have that part of South America that is now eastern Brazil.

Further expeditions by Spanish sailors and explorers increased European knowledge of the islands and the adjacent lands of Central America. Within 15 years the Spanish had defeated the poorly armed Amerindians (Carib and Arawak peoples) and had gained control over a large part of the Caribbean. Spanish settlements were established in Cuba and Puerto Rico. In the 1520s Spanish *conquistadores*, with their guns, armour and horses, subjugated the powerful Aztec state in central Mexico. By 1540 they had also defeated the Inca Empire on the slopes of the Andes of Peru. Although Spain now claimed most of the American continent, both north and south, her effective control was limited to relatively small areas of the Caribbean, and the coastline of South America.

South and Central America became a great treasure-house of silver and gold for Spain. She attempted to exclude from her new empire all other European states and traders and to preserve a complete monopoly. The wealth of the conquered provinces, stripped from the defeated Amerindians and dug from mines, was shipped to Spain, which grew strong both economically and militarily. Amerindians were enslaved and forced to work in mines and on a small number of sugar plantations created by the Spaniards. Conditions were harsh and brutal and the Amerindians, not used to such work, died in large numbers. The arrival of the Spaniards in America led not only to military conquest but to

the introduction of fatal diseases. The peoples of America, for long isolated from the rest of the world, lacked immunity towards many of the diseases brought by the Europeans, such as smallpox, measles, and influenza. As a result, millions died. For example, it is estimated that the population of Mexico, which numbered 20 million in 1520, was reduced to little more than one million by 1600.

Some Christian priests tried to prevent the

African slaves were employed by the Portuguese in Brazil to mine gold, silver and diamonds. The work was hard and the Black slaves were brutally treated. An Italian missionary who visited the country in 1682 was told that "their labour is so hard and their sustenance so small, that they are reckoned to live long if they hold out seven years". Because of their poor health Black slaves had few children. Thus the Portuguese had to continue importing slave labour from Africa to work on the plantations and in the mines of Brazil.

Black slaves mining for gold in the Serro do Frio, Brazil.

enslavement of the Amerindians but they were strongly opposed by Spanish settlers who required labourers. Then Africa was suggested as an alternative source of slave labour; Africans were resistant to the diseases that were killing the Amerindians and their value as slaves was well known. In 1518 a Spanish ship landed the first Black slaves in America. Throughout the sixteenth century small numbers of Black slaves were shipped to the Americas. They were employed in the mines, on the small plantations and also as soldiers in the continuing Spanish conquest of the New World. By 1600 Blacks could be found in equal number throughout every province of Spanish America and 50 years later up to 150,000 African slaves had been landed in the Spanish and Portuguese colonies in America.

The Portuguese were well placed to take a major part in the early transatlantic trade in slaves. They had possessions in West and equatorial Africa, they controlled the Atlantic islands and also held the coast of Brazil. In addition, the Portuguese knew all about growing sugar, a crop that was ideally suited to the colony of Brazil. Sugar plantations were set up in Brazil increasingly after 1550 and African slaves imported as the labour force. Sugar became big business and other European states showed a growing interest in gaining tropical colonies in

An early sugar factory in the Caribbean. The cane is being grown on the right, cut and crushed by the large roller and then the juice extracted in the larger boiler in the front of the picture.

In 1655 Henry Whistler, an Englishman and a member of the expedition to conquer Jamaica, visited the English Caribbean island of Barbados where he observed the varied settlers. But what fascinated him most were the Black slaves brought from Africa:

This island is one of the richest spots of ground in the world and fully inhabited. But were the people suitable to the island, it were not to be compared. . . . The gentry here doth live far better than ours do in England. They have most of them 100 or 2 or 3 of slaves apes who they command as they please. Here they may say what they have is their own. And they have that liberty of conscience which we so long have in England fought for, but they do abuse it. This island is inhabited with all sorts: with English, French, Dutch, Scots, Irish, Spaniards they being Jews, with Indians and miserable Negroes born to perpetual slavery, they and their seed. These Negroes they do allow as many wives as they will have; some will have three or four, according as they find their body able. Our English here doth think a Negro child the first day it is born to be worth £5; they cost them nothing the bringing up, they go always naked. Some planters will have thirty more or less about four or five years old. They sell them from one to the other as we do sheep. This island is the dunghill whereon England doth cast forth its rubbish. Rogues and whores and such like people are those which are generally brought here. A rogue in England will hardly make a cheater here. A bawd brought over puts on a demure comportment; a whore if handsome makes a wife for some rich planter. But in plain, the island of itself is very delightful and pleasant.

Extracts from Henry Whistler's *Journal of the West Indian Expedition*, as adapted by Richard S. Dunn in *Sugar and Slaves. The Rise of the Planter Class in the English West Indies, 1624-1713*, Jonathan Cape, 1973, p. 77)

the Americas. The English, French, and Dutch raided both the Spanish and Portuguese possessions and by the early seventeenth century had gained control over many of the islands of the Caribbean. The English, for example, settled Barbados in 1627, Antigua in 1632, and captured Jamaica from the Spanish in 1655. For a brief period the Dutch held the fertile sugar- and coffee-growing lands of coastal Brazil, but they were finally retaken by the Portuguese in 1654. Spanish attempts to maintain a trading monopoly over its own possessions were also slowly undermined and ships of other European states increasingly dominated the shipping lanes to and from America.

In Europe during the late sixteenth and seventeenth centuries there was a growing demand for sugar. It was used for preserving fruit through the winter and for distilling and brewing, as well as in many household recipes such as cakes and biscuits. In the 1550s Europe's main sources of sugar were bees and the small cane plantations on the Mediterranean and Atlantic islands. The population of Europe was increasing and there was also a growing demand for sugar to sweeten drinks such as tea, coffee and cocoa.

In their newly acquired Caribbean island colonies the English, French and Dutch began to establish sugar plantations. Sugar production was labour intensive, requiring close to one labourer for every acre of cane. Many smaller plantation owners could not afford the machinery necessary for processing the cane into sugar and molasses and so sold their holdings to wealthier men, who thus became large plantation owners.

At first convicts and bondservants brought over from Europe worked the plantations. Bondservants agreed to work for a period of three to five years in return for a grant of land at the end of their "bond". But the work of sugar production was a hard, back-breaking grind, disliked and resisted by most Europeans. As the demand for sugar grew so did the need for a large and steady supply of cheap labour. This was to come from the shores of Africa.

From the 1650s onwards the number of Black slaves shipped across the Atlantic from Africa to the Americas rapidly increased. The slave trade became an important part of a risky but highly profitable triangular system of transatlantic trade. Manufactured goods produced in Europe were exchanged in West Africa for a variety of local

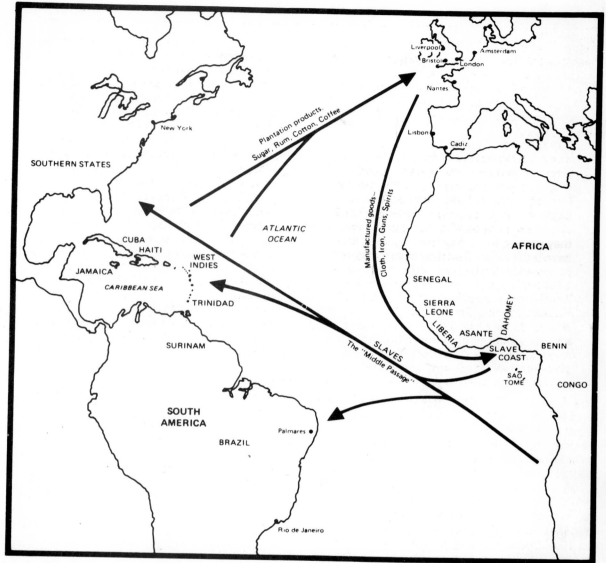

The triangular trade.

Landing African Slaves in Europe

A Portuguese writer in the fifteenth century described the arrival of African slaves at Lisbon:

> Some slaves kept their heads low and their faces bathed in tears, looking one upon another; others stood groaning, looking up to heaven, crying out loudly; others struck their faces with the palms of their hands, throwing themselves at full length upon the ground. But to increase their sufferings still more, there now arrived those who had charge of the division of the captives, and who began to separate one from another; and then was it needful to part fathers from sons, husbands from wives, brothers from brothers. No respect was shewn either to friends or relations, but each fell where his lot took him.

goods, but particularly slaves, who were then taken to the American colonies. In America the slaves were sold at a considerable profit. The ships were loaded with goods such as sugar, cotton and tobacco, which had been produced by slave labour. These would then be shipped to Europe, thus completing the triangle of trade.

Huge profits were made in this trading system by merchants, planters, and financiers. The African continent had become tied into an expanding world trading system that was increasingly dominated by Europeans and geared towards making large profits for certain groups of people in Africa, the Americas and western Europe.

5 The African Slave Trade

Slavery and the trade in slaves existed throughout Africa long before Europeans began to explore its coastline in the fifteenth century. Most African communities had slaves, although the way that they were treated and the kind of work they did varied greatly from one society to another. In some African polities, or states, Black slaves from other African states were highly regarded for their loyalty and provided soldiers and senior officials. However, as a rule, slaves did

---

Two Views of Slavery in West Africa

1. Domestic, or household, slaves

Those prisoners (of war) which were not sold or redeemed we kept as slaves: but how different was their condition from that of the slaves in the West Indies! With us they do no more work than other members of the community, even their master; their food, clothing and lodging were nearly the same as theirs . . . and there was scarce any other difference between them than a superior degree of importance which the head of a family possesses in our state, and that authority which, as such, he exercises over every part of his household. Some of our slaves even had slaves under them as their own property and for their own use.
(Olaudah Equiano, in his Autobiography published in 1789, describing slavery among the Igbo people)

The condition of the slave in the countries under our protection is by no means one of unmitigated hardship. In ordinary cases, the slave is considered as a member of his master's family, and often succeeds to his property, in default of a natural heir. He eats with him from the same dish, and has an equal share in all his simple enjoyments.
(Brodie Cruikshank, *Eighteen Years on the Gold Coast of Africa*, Vol. II, 1853)

2. Slave Labour in the Gold Mines of West Africa

The gold mines were seven in number. They are divided among seven kings, each of whom had one. The mines are dug very deeply into the ground. The kings have slaves whom they put in the mines and to whom they gave wives, and the wives the slaves take with them; and they bear and rear children in these mines. The kings, also, furnish them with food and drink.
(An account by a Portuguese traveller in the sixteenth century, quoted in Edward Reynolds, *Stand the Storm. A History of the Atlantic Slave Trade*, Allison & Busby, 1985, p. 8)

In the gold mines Asante slaves were forced to work underground. A Danish agent in the mid-eighteenth century described them as pits dug into the ground in a slanting manner. The pits were like a staircase with each step measuring about one metre high. On each step stood a slave who passed up the soil on trays and handed down the empty ones to men working at the face, who picked out the earth and extracted the ore. The pits varied in depth between four and ten metres. Slaves were also used to pan for gold on the banks of rivers. Joseph Dupuis, who visited Asante in 1820, reported:

on the banks of the Barra . . . during the season of rain . . . there is occupation for eight or ten thousand slaves for two months; and the metal they collect, added to the produce of the pits . . . now finds its way to Ashantee, from whence it passes in small quantities to the maritime provinces . . . is there alloyed before it reaches the hands of the whites.
(Joseph Dupuis, *Journal of Residence in Ashantee*, 1824, p. 1)

23

much of the back-breaking work of agriculture, while in the West African kingdom of Asante thousands of slaves were employed in the dangerous gold mines. Slaves in Asante could also be put to death as sacrifices in religious rituals. Olaudah Equiano argued that compared to plantation slavery in America the lot of a slave in Africa was relatively free and easy. There may be some truth in this. Perhaps the important thing to remember is that being a slave, whether in Africa or America, meant that you were owned by someone, regarded as inferior, and forced to work.

In the period before 1750 very few Europeans or Africans, except those unfortunate enough to be enslaved, thought that there was anything wrong with buying, selling and owning human beings. Those engaged in the slave trade in Africa and across the Atlantic to the Americas saw it like any other trade. Profit was their main interest, not questions about morality. Africa was just another source of trade goods to be bought and sold. Goods such as ivory, gum, gold, spices, timber, and also slaves were available for exchange for the manufactured cloth, ironwares, liquor, beads, firearms and gunpowder that were

Willem Bosman, a Dutch trader, worked on the Gold Coast in the last few years of the seventeenth century. He wrote letters home to his uncle describing how slaves were bought and sold:

When the slaves which are brought from the inland countries come to Whidah, they are put in prison together, when we treat concerning buying them, they are all brought out together in a large plain, where, by our surgeons, they are thoroughly examined, and that naked both men and women, without the least distinction or modesty. Those which are approved as good are set on one side; in the meanwhile a burning iron, with the arm or name of the company, lies in the fire, with which ours are marked on the breast when we have agreed with the owners of the slaves they are returned to their prisons, where, from that time forward, they are kept at our charge, and cost us two pence a day each slave, which serves to subsist them like criminals on bread and water.

(Willem Bosman, *A New and Accurate Description of the Coast of Guinea*, London, 1705, p. 310)

A European merchant bargaining the price of slaves and trade goods on the West African coast. From an early nineteenth-century watercolour.

An eighteenth-century engraving showing a European trader branding a slave with the mark of the trading company.

The Slave Trade and British Prosperity

But is it not well-known that the business of planting in our British Colonies, as well as in the French, is carried on by the labour of negroes, imported from Africa? Are we not indebted to the Africans, for our sugar, tobacco, rice, rum, and all other plantation produce? And the greater the number of negroes imported into our colonies, from Africa, will not the exportation of British manufactures among the Africans be in proportion; they being paid for in such commodities only? The more our plantations abound in negroes, will not more land become cultivated, and both better and greater variety of plantation commodities be produced? May we not therefore say . . . that the general navigation of Great Britain owes all its increase and splendour to the commerce of its American and African colonies; and that it cannot be maintained and enlarged otherwise than from the constant prosperity of both those branches, whose interests are mutual and inseparable?

(Malachi Postlethwayt, *African Trade, the Great Pillar and Support of the British Plantation Trade in North America*, 1745)

Many of the dealers in slaves living on the West coast of Africa were Afro-Europeans, or *mulattos*. They were the result of sexual encounters between European sailors and traders and African women. Many *mulatto* traders had close contacts with African rulers and also the Europeans in the forts. One important *mulatto* trader on the coast of Sierra Leone was Henry Tucker. An Irish slaver by the name of Nick Owen, who started trading in slaves in that area in 1754, described Tucker as

> . . . a man who had acquired a great fortune by his skill and some other abilities in the way of trade. . . . He has been in England, Spain and Portugal and is master of the English tongue; he has six or seven wives and numerous offspring of sons and daughters; his strength consists of his own slaves and their children, who have built a town about him and serve as his *gremetos* [retainers] upon all occasions. This man bears the character of a fair trader among the Europeans, but to the contrary among the blacks. His riches set him above the Kings and his numerous people above being surprised by war; almost all the blacks owe him money, which brings a dread of being stepped upon that account, so that he is esteemed and feared by all who have the misfortune to be in his power.

(Quoted in Eveline C. Martin, ed., *Journal of a Slave-Dealer, 1754-1759*, 1930, p. 76)

brought from Europe, India and North America. Africans and Europeans were equally involved in the slave trade; it was a trade of mutual advantage.

Europeans came to the coast of Africa as traders and not as settlers. Few White men ventured far inland; it was unhealthy and they were there to buy and sell goods, not to explore. The trade routes, both long- and short-distance routes connecting different market centres together, were all controlled by Africans. African middlemen jealously guarded their short-distance trade routes to the coast and their source of supplies from other Africans and also from any European competition.

The slaves brought down to the coast for sale were gained by various means. Many were prisoners captured during wars. The kingdom of Asante had a regular supply of slaves sent as tribute from the northern provinces that it had conquered. Some of these slaves were used within Asante but large numbers were brought down to the sea for sale to the Europeans. Slaves were also kidnapped, or "panyarred" by merchants, although states often raided their weaker neighbours in order to seize people as slaves. Firearms and gunpowder played an important part in this. Forest states, such as Asante and Dahomey, which by the eighteenth century had gained control of part of the coast and had entered into direct trade with Europeans, were thus able to buy weapons and build up their military strength and extend their imperial possessions. Another source of slaves was criminals and those people unfortunate enough to have got themselves involved in debts that they could not repay.

A Slave Caravan Travelling to the Coast of West Africa

Mungo Park, the Scottish traveller, embarked on a 500-mile journey with such a caravan in 1796.

A slave caravan. From a nineteenth-century engraving.

The slaves which Karfa had brought with him were all of them prisoners of war . . . they viewed me at first with looks of horror, and repeatedly asked if my countrymen were cannibals. A deeply rooted idea, that the whites purchase Negroes for the purpose of eating them, or of selling them to others, that they may be eaten, makes the slaves contemplate a journey towards the Coast with great terror; insomuch that the merchants are forced to keep them constantly in irons, and watch them very closely, to prevent their escape. They are commonly secured by putting the right leg of one and the left of another, into the same pair of fetters. By supporting the fetters with a string, they can walk though very slowly. Every four slaves are likewise fastened together by the necks, with a strong rope of twisted thongs; and in the night, an additional pair of fetters is put on their hands, and sometimes a light chain passed round their necks.

(Mungo Park, *Travels in the Interior Districts of Africa, 1795-97*, 1798)

The arrival of Europeans on the coast gave the African slave trade a new dimension and direction. First of all, Europeans opened up new sources of supply for slaves and also new slave routes within Africa. The Portuguese, for example, shipped slaves from their island of São Tomé to Elmina on the Gold Coast, where they sold them to Africans for use in the local gold mines. Secondly, the Europeans provided an overseas market for slaves, initially to southern Europe, and then, after 1520, to the Americas. In the early years the transatlantic slave trade took from Africa only a few thousand slaves per year. These numbers rapidly increased in the latter half of the seventeenth century, as more and more European states became involved in the

John Newton was the captain of a slave ship trading on the coast of West Africa in the mid-eighteenth century. Newton kept a log in which he described his daily activities. At first he thought there was nothing wrong with slaving. In one entry to his journal he says: "I thank God for a creditable way of life." However, he became disgusted with the slave trade and campaigned to end it. Here he describes the various methods used by European traders to defraud Africans. In fact, both Africans and Europeans tried to defraud each other.

Not an article that is capable of diminution or adulteration, is delivered genuine, or entire. The spirits are lowered by water. False heads are put into the kegs that contain the gun powder; so that, though the keg appears large there is not more powder in it, than in a much smaller one. The linen and cotton cloths are opened, and two or three yards, according to the length of the piece, cut off, not from the end, but out of the middle, where it is not readily noticed. The natives are cheated, in the number, weight, measure, or quality of what they purchase, in every possible way; and by habit and emulation, a marvellous dexterity is acquired in these practices. And thus the natives in their turn, in proportion to their commerce with the Europeans, and (I am sorry to add) particularly with the English, become jealous, insidious and revengeful.
(Quoted in Bernard Martin and Mark Spurrell, eds., *The Journal of a Slave Trader 1750-1754*, Epworth Press, 1962, p. 106)

barbarous business. During the eighteenth century, when the plantation system in the Caribbean reached its peak, more than six million Black slaves were shipped out of Africa for America.

At the African end the business of selling slaves was conducted between African middlemen and a European factor, or agent, who lived on the coast and looked after the interests of a European trading company. He usually lived in a defended warehouse or fort. Many of the African middlemen were Afro-Europeans, or *mulattos*, who commonly used Portuguese as the language of trade. Slaves were brought to the coast in ones or twos, or in long columns, or coffles, roped and chained together. They were held in stockades or *baracoons*, while the lengthy bargaining over prices and the exchange of goods was conducted with the European factor. When possible he bought only healthy strong slaves. Young men who could be turned into plantation labourers commanded a good price. So did young women who could be used for breeding more slaves in America.

As the European factor bought slaves he locked them in the warehouse or fort. The slaves might stay there for several months while a full cargo was gathered together and a suitable ship appeared.

The island of Goreé was a major slaving centre on the coast of West Africa. The European merchant lived upstairs in this house while the slaves were kept locked up in rooms beneath. When a ship arrived the slaves were taken through the door straight into boats and carried out to the waiting slaver.

6 The Middle Passage

The second leg of the triangular trade, shipping slaves from Africa to America, was known as the "middle passage". The length of the journey depended on wind and weather and the distance to be travelled. Given good sailing conditions a ship could leave the Gambia and reach the most easterly islands of the Caribbean, a distance of 5100 km, within 40 days. On the other hand, a ship coming from Angola and bound for Jamaica or New Orleans would have to travel 9600 km. Longer voyages meant higher risks. If a ship was becalmed or driven off course and food and water ran low then it was much more likely that slaves would die.

Slave ships, or slavers, varied in size from 40 to 400 tons. Many were owned or charted by companies backed by investors who provided the outward cargo for sale on the African coast and who hoped to make a large profit from each part of the triangular trade. It was a risky business but large profits could be made from a single voyage. The Liverpool slaver *Thomas* in 1767 made an overall profit of £24,000 on a single voyage although 100 of the 630 slaves on board died before the ship reached Kingston in Jamaica.

Before being taken on board, slaves were often branded, had their heads shaved, and their few clothes removed. This was done to prevent disease being brought on board. Very often male and female slaves were put into separate holds. Chained together in the dark space below decks

Loading slaves on the West Coast of Africa. From a nineteenth-century engraving.

Expenses Out

Cost of *La Fortuna*, a 90-ton schooner	$ 3,700.000
Fitting out, sails, carpenter and cooper's bills	2,500.00
Provisions for crew and slaves	1,115.00
Wages advanced to 18 men before the mast	900.00
Wages advanced to captain, mates, boatswain, cook and steward	440.00
200,000 cigars and 500 doubloons, cargo	10,900.00
Clearance and hush money	200.00
	19,755.00
Commission at 5 per cent	987.00
Full cost of voyage out	$20,742.00

Expenses Home

Captain's head money at $8 a head	$ 1,746.00
Mate's head money at $4 a head	873.00
Second mate's and boatswain's head money at $2 each	873.00
Captain's wages	219.78
First mate's wages	175.56
Second mate's and boatswain's wages	307.12
Cook and steward's wages	264.00
Eighteen sailors' wages	1,972.00
	$27,172.46

Expenses in Havana

Government officers at $8 per head	$ 1,736.00
My commission on 217 slaves, Expenses off	5,565.00
Consignees' commissions	3,873.00
217 slave dresses at $2 each	634.00
Extra expenses of all kinds	1,000.00
Total expense	$39,980.46

Returns

Value of vessel at auction	$ 3,950.00
Proceeds of 217 slaves	77,469.00
	81,419.00
Expenses	39,980.46
Net profit	$41,438.54

(Brantz Mayer, *Captain Canot or Twenty Years of an African Slaver*, 1866, p. 101)

Slaving was a risky but profitable business. Ships might be wrecked or lose their cargoes of goods and slaves from storm, lack of wind, or mutiny. After the slave trade was made illegal in 1807 slave ship owners ran the risk of being stopped, having their cargoes confiscated and their ships destroyed. Nevertheless, the slave trade continued and large profits could still be made. In 1854 Brantz Mayer wrote a popular and sensational book about the slave trade. He claimed the book was based on the journal and memoirs of Captain Canot. Here are Canot's accounts for a slaving expedition in the schooner *La Fortuna* in 1827 from Cuba to the west coast of Africa.

Slaves being brought aboard a slaver off the coast of West Africa to be chained and put below decks.

Account by Captain Thomas Phillips of the voyage of the slaver *Hannibal* from West Africa to the West Indies, 1693.

When our slaves are aboad we shackle the men two and two, while we lie in port, and in sight of their own country, for 'tis then they attempt to make their escape, and mutiny; to prevent which we always keep sentinels upon the hatchways, and have a chest full of small arms, ready loaded and prim'd, constantly lying at hand upon the quarter-deck, together with some granada shells; and two of our quarter-deck guns, pointing on the deck thence, and two more out of the steerage, and the door of which is always kept shut, and well barr'd.

They are fed twice a day, at ten in the morning, and four in the evening, which is the time they are aptest to mutiny, being all upon deck; therefore all that time, what of our men are not employed in distributing their food to them, and settling them stand to their arms. Their chief diet is call'd dabbadabb, being Indian corn ground as small as oat-meal, mix'd with water, and boiled well in a large copper furnace, till 'tis as thick as a pudding, about a peckful of which is allow'd to ten men, with a little salt, and palm oil to relish. Three days a week they have horse-beans boil'd for their dinner and supper; these beans the Negroes extremely love and desire,

beating their breast eating them and crying Pram! Pram! which is Very good! They are indeed the best diet for them, having a binding quality, and consequently good to prevent the flux, which is the distemper that most affects them, and ruins our voyages by their deaths.

We often at sea in the evening would let the slaves come up into the sun to air themselves, and make them jump and dance for an hour or two to our bag-pipes, harp, and fiddle, by which exercise to preserve them in health; but notwithstanding all our endeavour, 'twas my hard fortune to have great sickness and mortality among them.

We spent in our passage from St Thomas to Barbadoes two months eleven days, from 25 August to 4 November following: in which time there happen'd much sickness and mortality among my poor men and Negroes, that of the first we buried fourteen, and of the last, 320 which was a great detriment to our voyage, the royal African company losing ten pounds by every slave that died, and the owners of the ship ten pounds ten shillings, being the freight agreed on to be paid them by the charter-party for every Negroe delivered alive ashore to the African company's agents at Barbadoes; whereby the loss in all amounted to near 6560 pounds sterling.

(Quoted in John Churchill, *A Collection of Voyages and Travels*, Vol. VI, 1746, p. 231)

the slaves were cramped together tightly "like books upon a shelf" or, as one captain put it, "with not so much room to move as a man in his coffin". On some slavers extra bulkheads were built to divide the ship and give the crew more control over the slaves.

Once the ship was out at sea slaves could be brought up on deck, usually a few at a time, to be fed and for exercise. Some slaves refused to eat and had to be forced. Those who would not exercise on deck to keep fit were whipped. Many slaves experienced deep despair. Some just died; others killed themselves. Nets were spread along the side of the ship to prevent slaves jumping overboard at exercise time, but Olaudah Equiano describes two men who "preferring death to such a life of misery, somehow made through the netting and jumped into the sea". The crew often mistreated the slaves, particularly the women, who were sexually abused.

The crew of a slaver always had to be on guard in case the slaves should attempt to seize the ship. Troublesome slaves were kept in chains and closely watched. Although the ship's crew had access to guns there were times when determined slaves broke out of the hold, over-powered the sailors and took over the slaver. One famous instance was the "mutiny" on the Spanish schooner *Amistad* in 1839. The slaves killed the captain and most of the crew, some of whom were Black, and took control of the ship as it sailed from Cuba. But they were unable to work the schooner, which drifted north off the coast of the United States. Food and water ran low and eventually the U.S. authorities boarded the ship off New England.

Many slaves died on the middle passage from diseases, sickness, harsh treatment, and poor food. So did many of the crew, especially from diseases caught off the West African coast or on the middle passage. There is no way of knowing how many slaves died on the dreadful voyages across the Atlantic. But we do have some sets of fairly accurate figures for certain periods and various estimates. For example, between 1680 and 1688 the 249 ships of the Royal African Company carried 60,783 slaves, of whom only 45,396 survived the voyage, a death rate of 24 per cent. This very high figure of mortality in the seventeenth century declined during the next 100 years and by the 1790s many slavers were reaching America without the loss of a single

A slave mutiny was a constant fear of the crew of a slaver. Few slave mutinies at sea were successful. Even if the slaves did succeed in seizing the ship they would not be able to sail it.

slave. Nevertheless, during the whole period of the transatlantic slave trade, from 1520 to 1860, perhaps 15-16 per cent of slaves died during the middle passage. The figure is increased by possibly 5 per cent if we also add those who died or were killed while being brought to the coast of Africa for sale. The slave trade was in every way a brutal and bloody commerce.

Captains of slave ships had an interest in keeping alive as many slaves as possible; more slaves landed in America meant higher profits. They tried, therefore, not to buy sick slaves in Africa but, inevitably, some diseased men and women were brought on board, making the whole human cargo at risk. Captain Canot, a nineteenth-century slaver, described discovering among his slaves a young boy with smallpox; he poisoned the child and threw his body overboard in order to protect his cargo and crew.

Towards the end of the middle passage, as the port of landing hove in sight, the slaves were prepared for sale. It was important that they looked fit and healthy. They received a thorough wash on deck and several good meals. Their bodies might then be rubbed over with olive oil to make their skins shine so they would look their best when they were put up for sale.

If at the first port of call the price of slaves was

A Brazilian Slaver

Robert Walsh, a British clergyman who lived in Brazil in 1828-9, describes a British naval ship stopping a Brazilian slaver in the Atlantic Ocean.

When we mounted her decks, we found her full of slaves. She was called the *Veloz*, commanded by Captain José Barbosa, bound to Bahia. She was a very broad-decked ship, with a mainmast, schooner-rigged, and behind her foremast was that large formidable gun, which turned on a broad circle of iron, on deck, and which enabled her to act as a pirate, if her slaving speculation had failed. She had taken in, on the coast of Africa, 336 males, and 226 females, making in all 562, and had been out seventeen days, during which she had thrown overboard fifty-five. The slaves were all enclosed under grated hatchways, between decks. The space was so low, that they sat between each other's legs, and stowed so close together, that there was no possibility of their lying down, or at all changing their position, by night or day. As they belonged to, and were shipped on account of different individuals, they were all branded, like sheep, with the owners' marks of different forms. These were impressed under their breasts, or on their arms, and, as the mate informed me, with perfect indifference, "queimados pelo ferro quento – burnt with the red-hot iron." Over the hatchway stood a ferocious looking fellow, with a scourge of many twisted thongs in his hand, who was the slave-driver of the ship, and whenever he heard the slightest noise below, he shook it over them, and seemed eager to exercise it. . . .

But the circumstance which struck us most forcibly, was, how it was possible for such a number of human beings to exist, packed up and wedged together as tight as they could cram, in low cells, three feet high, the greater part of which, except that immediately under the grated hatchways, was shut out from light or air, and this when the thermometer, exposed to the open sky, was standing in the shade, on our deck, at 89°. The space between decks was divided into two compartments, 3 feet 3 inches high; the size of one was 16 feet by 18, and of the other 40 by 21; into the first were crammed the women and girls; into the second, the men and boys: 226 fellow-creatures were thus thrust into one space 288 feet square; and 336 into another space 800 square feet, giving to the whole an average of 23 inches, and to each woman not more than 13 inches, though many of them were pregnant.

(Robert Walsh, *Notices of Brazil in 1828 and 1829*, 1831)

The Number of Slaves and the Death Rate on the Middle Passage

How many slaves were shipped out of Africa in the period of the transatlantic slave trade? Recent studies suggest the figures shown below.

Of these, it is estimated that between 1520 and 1860 about 16 per cent died during the middle passage.

Graph to show the annual average number of slaves leaving Africa between 1450 and 1870.

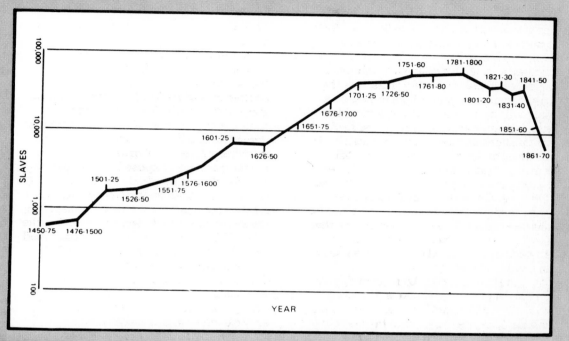

too low the captain might move on to other ports looking for better sales. Slaves were sold in three ways: by public auction, private treaty, and by "scramble". In a "scramble" the slaves were placed within a fenced area. At a given signal bidders seized the slaves that they wanted and then negotiated the price for each one. In the early years of the trade the ship's captain received sugar and rum in exchange for his slaves. But by the eighteenth century payment was made in bills of exchange which could be cashed elsewhere in America or in Europe.

An early nineteenth-century poster advertising slaves for sale.

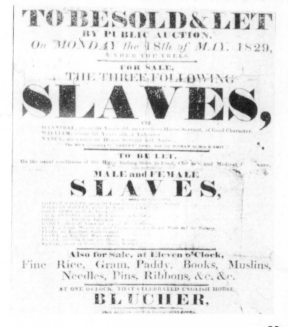

Estimated Slave Imports into the Americas, 1451-1870 (in thousands)

Region	1451-1600	1601-1700	1701-1810	1811-70	Total
British North America	—	—	348.0	51.0	399.0
Spanish America	75.0	292.5	578.6	606.0	1552.1
British Caribbean	—	263.7	1401.3	—	1552.1
French Caribbean	—	155.8	1348.4	.96.0	1600.2
Dutch Caribbean	—	40.0	460.0	—	500.0
Danish Caribbean	—	4.0	24.0	—	28.0
Brazil	50.0	560.0	1891.4	1145.4	3646.8
Europe	149.9	25.1			175.0
Atlantic islands	101.1	23.9			125.0
Total	376	1365	6051.7	1898.4	9578.2

(N.B. These figures need to be taken as within ± 10 per cent)

It is difficult to give an accurate estimate of slave deaths on the middle passage, but some records do exist, such as these from the French slaving town of Nantes for the eighteenth century:

Period	Deaths from disease (%)	Deaths from all causes (%)
1715-19	12.2	19.1
1720-24	19.1	22.4
1727-31	13.5	13.5
1732-36	18.4	18.4
1737-41	19.4	19.6
1742-45	11.1	16.8
1746-50	10.8	11.5
1751-55	15.8	15.8
1756-63	5.9	7.9
1764-68	13.2	13.2
1769-73	14.2	14.8
1774-75	14.5	16.2

(Gaston Martin, *Nantes au XVIIIe Siecle: L'Ere des Negriers, 1714-1774*, Paris, 1931, p. 15)

7 Slavery in the Americas

On arrival in America slaves were sold usually by some form of auction. The youngest and fittest slaves, known as "prime" slaves reached the highest prices and usually went first; the sick and older slaves, known as "refuse" slaves, sold last and at lower prices. The price of a "prime" slave varied. Much depended on the state of the economy and the supply of Black slaves. When the slave trade became illegal in many parts of America in the early nineteenth century the price of slaves tended to rise.

In the American colonies slaves were regarded as items of private property. One law called them "chattels personal". They could be bought and sold just like farm animals and pieces of furniture. Families could be split up and parents might never see their children again. Certainly some slave owners did attempt to keep families together but it was quite common for slaves to be advertised in this way:

> NEGROES FOR SALE – A negro woman, twenty-four years of age, and her two children, one eight and the other three years old. Said negroes will be sold SEPARATELY or together, *as desired*. The woman is a good seamstress. She will be sold low for cash, or EXCHANGED FOR GROCERIES.
> For terms, apply to MATTHEW BLISS & CO., 1 Front Levee.
> (*New Orleans Bee*, March 1858)

Many slave owners regarded their slaves as items of property on which they could put a specific price. The value of a slave depended on the work he or she was capable of doing on the plantation, in the home, or in the workshop.

Although there were poor Whites in the Americas, generally only Blacks were slaves. People of African origin were Black and their colour identified them in the eyes of Whites as inferior. But if we look more closely at the population of the slave-owning communities we see a fairly complex picture of pigmentation.

These notices, from a newspaper published in Memphis, Tennessee, in 1858, clearly show the way in which slaves were regarded and treated as items of property, to be advertised and sold in exactly the same way as cotton, sweets or tobacco.

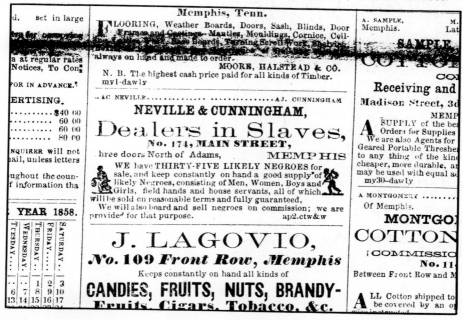

A slave family up for auction in the United States during the mid-nineteenth century. Members of families might be sold separately, although some slave owners tried to keep parents and children together because that prevented slaves becoming even more desperate and discontented.

in most slave-owning communities some Blacks were free; in some cases free Blacks owned Black slaves.

Most slave colonies had laws regulating how slaves should be treated. Laws recognized that slaves could be private property but at the same time they also acknowledged that slaves were "persons". As persons they had to be treated in a reasonably humane way (slave owners could not just kill their slaves) and slaves could also be held responsible for their actions. So at one level the law treated Black slaves as property but at another level as human beings. The Dutch, French, Portuguese, Spanish, British, and Dutch all had slave laws. Some historians have argued that the harshest laws were those of the Dutch and the British while the most lenient and less colour-conscious were those of the Portuguese. There is some truth in this but in all systems of slavery the slave was unfree and thought of as inferior and an item of property.

New slaves had to be "seasoned", or broken in, to their work. During this time many slaves died. Disobedience was punished by whipping. Obstinate and troublesome slaves were chained

---

The master may sell him, dispose of his person, his industry, and his labour: he can do nothing, possess nothing, nor acquire anything but what must belong to his master.
(The Slave Code of the State of Louisiana)

The Christian Church in eighteenth-century America supported slavery. This is part of a sermon to slaves by a Bishop of Virginia:

Almighty God hath been pleased to make you slaves here, and give you nothing but labour and poverty in this world, which you are obliged to submit to as it is His will that it should be so. Your bodies, you know, are not your own: they are at the disposal of those who you belong to.

There were people of various shades of colour and physical appearance and it was not always easy to identify whether an individual was Black or White, or perhaps we should say *more* Black or *less* Black. Although Black slaves predominated

---

Edward Long was born in England in 1734 and lived in the British slave colony of Jamaica from 1757 to 1769. By marriage he was connected to the largest slave-owning families in the island. Long believed that people could be placed in order according to the position "God had given them"; at the top were the White races and at the bottom Africans, who were little higher than animals.

In many respects they [the Blacks] are more like beasts than men; their complexion is dark, they are short and thick-set; their noses flat, like those of a Dutch dog; their lips very thick and big; their teeth exceedingly white, but very long, and ill set, some of them sticking out of their mouths like boar tusks. . . . Their hearing is remarkably quick; their faculties of smell and taste are truly bestial, no less so their commerce with the other sex; in these acts they are libidinous and shameless as monkeys, or baboons.
(Edward Long, History of Jamaica, Vol. II, 1774, pp. 364-5 and 383)

Black slave children and the White master's children might play together, but inter-racial friendship rarely survived beyond childhood in the climate of prejudice that existed over much of the United States in the nineteenth century.

up and sometimes mutilated by being branded or having their ears cut off. We also now know from recent studies of the diet and health of slaves in the Caribbean that they were often underfed and overworked, so that many died as a result of neglect and ill-treatment.

On the islands in the Caribbean, in Brazil and the southern states of the United States large numbers of slaves worked on the plantations, growing and processing sugar, coffee, cotton and tobacco. This was labour-intensive work, cutting cane and picking cotton. Very few machines or animals were used in any part of the process; virtually all the work was done by human beings. On a cotton plantation in Mississippi the slaves woke before daylight. By first light they were at work and continued all day until dusk. Slaves might never leave a large plantation; it was like a separate world where they spent their whole lives.

Other slaves worked in mines, as domestic labour, as clerks, as seamen and in various crafts – as masons, coopers, carpenters and bricklayers. Domestic slaves ran White

Olaudah Equiano, who was a slave in the British West Indian islands in the 1750s-60s, described the brutal treatment given to some slaves:

> It was very common in several of the islands, particularly in St Kitt's, for the slaves to be branded with the initial letter of their master's name, and a load of heavy iron hooks hung about their necks. Indeed on the most trifling occasions they were loaded with chains, and often instruments of torture were added. The iron muzzle, thumbscrews, etc. are so well known as not to need a description, and were sometimes applied for the slightest faults. I have seen a negro beaten till some of his bones were broken for even letting a pot boil over. It is not surprising that usage like this should drive the poor creatures to despair and make them seek refuge in death from those evils which render their lives intolerable . . .
> (*Equiano's Travels*, first published 1789; abridged version edited by Paul Edwards, Heinemann Educational Books, 1967, p. 68)

Slave Labour in Brazil in the Nineteenth Century

The negro is not only the field labourer, but also the mechanic; not only hews the wood and draws the water, but by the skill of his hands contributes to fashion the luxuries of civilized life. The Brazilian employs him on all occasions, and in every possible way; – from fulfilling the office of valet and cook, to serving the purposes of the horse; from forming the gaudy trinkets, and shaping the costume which is to clothe and decorate his person, to discharging the vilest of servile duties.

(Thomas Nelson, *Remarks on Slavery and the Slave Trade of the Brazils*, London, 1846)

households and Black female slaves looked after the children of their owners. In the southern states of the United States in the nineteenth century as many as 10 per cent of slaves worked in factories and workshops. There were Black slaves in towns as well and they were probably treated far better than the vast majority of slaves who worked in the rural areas.

The day-to-day management of a large plantation was usually the task of a White overseer. The wealthy owners might live in the large house or mansion on the estate or in a nearby town. Many of those who amassed great wealth from the slave production of sugar in the Caribbean islands lived in elegant comfort on estates in Britain or France. A small handful of wealthy Whites dominated most of the slave-owning communities. In the Caribbean islands and the southern states of the United States the large plantation owners – the "planters" – had great power and influence. Planters in the British West Indies were so powerful that they could influence affairs in London 3000 miles away.

How many Black slaves were there in the Americas? Slaves came from two sources: they were imported across the Atlantic from Africa, and they were also the result of natural increase. In the seventeenth and eighteenth centuries the Black population of the Caribbean islands and Brazil increased mainly due to imports of slaves from Africa. As sugar boomed more slaves were required and imports grew rapidly. In 1670 there

Three illustrations from a nineteenth-century book by Richard Brigdens, West Indian Scenery with Illustrations of Negro Character, the Process of Making Sugar, etc., *published in 1836, showing planting the sugar cane, cutting canes and interior of a boiling-house.*

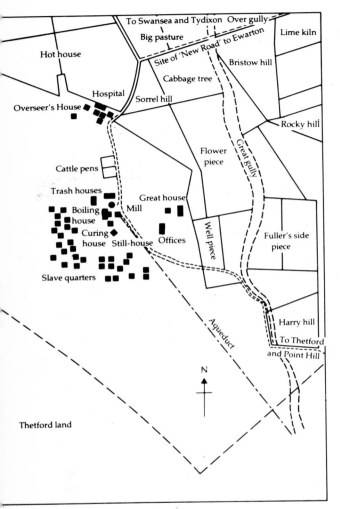

To Swansea and Tydixon Over gully
Big pasture
Site of 'New Road' to Ewarton
Lime kiln
Hot house
Bristow hill
Hospital
Cabbage tree
Overseer's House
Sorrel hill
Rocky hill
Flower piece
Great gully
Cattle pens
Trash houses
Great house
Boiling house
Mill
Curing house
Still-house
Offices
Well piece
Fuller's side piece
Slave quarters
Aqueduct
Harry hill
To Thetford and Point Hill
N
Thetford land

A plan of Worthy Park, Jamaica in 1794. This sugar plantation was in St John's Parish in the centre of the island and covered over 600 hectares. Generally the most valuable part of a plantation were the slaves. A plantation not only grew crops but it also had an industrial sector which processed what was grown. On this plan can be seen the mill for crushing the sugar and the boiling and curing houses. The slaves' quarters are near to the fields and well away from the Great House.

The Long Day of a Plantation Slave in the United States in the Nineteenth Century

An hour before daylight the horn is blown. Then the slaves arouse, prepare their breakfast, fill a gourd with water, in another, deposit their dinner of cold bacon and corn cake, and hurry to the field again. It is an offence invariably followed by a flogging to be found at the quarters after daybreak. Then the fears and labours of another day begin and until its close there is no such thing as rest.

... with the exception of ten or fifteen minutes, which is given them at noon to swallow their allowance of cold bacon, they are not permitted to be a moment idle until it is too dark to see, and when the moon is full, they oftentimes labour till the middle of the night. They do not dare to stop even at dinner time, nor return to the quarters, however late it be, until the order to halt is given by the driver.

(Solomon Northup, *Twelve Years a Slave*, 1853)

were 7000 Black slaves in Jamaica, about the same number as Whites, but by 1713 Blacks numbered 55,000 and Whites only 7000. Cuba's sugar industry expanded in the late eighteenth century and so did slave imports; in 1774 slaves formed 25 per cent of the total population but by 1827 they were 40 per cent. In many slave-owning communities Blacks outnumbered the Whites several times over, a cause of continual concern for the slave owners who feared that the Blacks might rise in revolt.

The second source of slaves was by natural increase – the children of slaves born and bred in America. Such children often were automatically slaves themselves. In the United States the slave population grew mainly in this way. Fewer than 400,000 slaves were imported into North America and the slave trade was declared illegal in 1808 but by 1860 the Black population had reached 4 million.

8 Slave Resistance and Revolts

Blacks resented and resisted slavery at every turn. In Africa they fought against those who attempted to capture them. On the voyage to America they sometimes seized the ship. And in the Americas, despite the attempts to break the spirit of slaves, they continued to resist in various ways. In many ways slaves could be very "troublesome property".

Some slaves meekly accepted their lot. But many protested in the easiest way they could. They pretended to be stupid and not to understand orders; slaves worked slowly, left farm gates open, stole or "lost" tools, or broke machinery on purpose. In fact, slaves used every device they could to show how deeply they hated their position and the way that they were treated.

Some slaves were bolder, going beyond this constant and subtle kind of protest, and managed to escape from their owners. This was more difficult in some of the smaller islands of the Caribbean because there were few places where a slave could hide successfully. However, in the larger islands like Jamaica and Cuba, or in Brazil and the southern states of the United States, slaves fled to remote and inaccessible regions such as mountains, forests, and swamp lands.

Towns and ships also often provided a safe refuge where runaway slaves could escape detection and find work.

Runaway slaves were hunted down by armed men with dogs. When caught they might be harshly flogged and forced to work in chains. Those who repeatedly tried to escape might be mutilated, for example have their foot cut off, or even be killed as a warning to other slaves.

Many of the runaways who reached wild country lived an independent existence. In the forests of Brazil in the seventeeth century bands of escaped Blacks set up an independent state known as Palmares. This African state was able to feed its population of 10,000 people and also to defend itself against repeated attacks by the Dutch and Portuguese. Finally in 1694, after 50 years of independence, Palmares fell to the Portuguese after a long siege. The Blacks were either killed or taken back into captivity.

Runaway slaves in Jamaica tried to escape to

Run Away

The following advertisement appeared in the *Daily Advertiser*, Kingston, Jamaica on 24 December, 1790.

Adam, a creole, a fisherman by trade, much pitted in the face with the small pox, short and well made, and will attempt to pass for free; being a great smatterer in religious topics, has been lately converted by Parson Lisle, and is always preaching or praying: he was seen on board a ship this morning, going to Old Harbour, and no doubt will sail out with her when she is completely loaded...

Runaway slaves, or those whom owners feared might try to escape, were often forced to wear a barbarous iron collar like this one to deter escape. The prongs were often a metre in length and prevented the slave from lying down. Originally designed for use in West Africa, the hooks on the end of each prong would entangle the escaping slave in trees and bushes.

the jagged limestone mountains in the centre of the island, where they could be out of reach of the White owners and government. From their mountain strongholds groups of escaped slaves, known as Maroons, waged guerilla war on the British. They became such a serious threat that following the unsuccessful attempt to defeat them in the first Maroon War of 1725-39 the British signed a treaty recognizing their independence. In the Dutch colony of Surinam slaves escaped into the jungles and established villages similar to those they had left in Africa. Raids were made on the coastal plantations and despite several expeditions the Dutch were unable to defeat the "Bush Negroes". Eventually, in 1825, the Dutch signed a treaty guaranteeing the freedom of the Blacks in the Bush in exchange for an agreement that the Blacks would stop raiding the plantations. Also, like the Maroons of Jamaica, they agreed to hand over to the Dutch any slaves who escaped to them. Today, the Maroons have been absorbed into the population of Jamaica but the "Bush Negroes" of Surinam live apart from other Blacks and have a culture which includes many African words, art forms and religious practices and customs.

The Maroons and the British agree to a treaty in the mid-eighteenth century. This engraving from an eighteenth-century source shows the Maroons as nearly naked, although it is likely that they wore more clothes than this.

Palmares

The African state of Palmares in Brazil was formed by runaway slaves. The most detailed first-hand accounts of Palmares are provided by Captain Fernao Carilho, a Portuguese officer who led expeditions against the Black stronghold between 1672 and 1680. This account comes from his reports written in 1676-77:

> The King of Palmares is called *Ganga-Zumba*, which means Great Lord; he has a large palace and he is assisted by guards and officials. He is treated with all respect due to a monarch. Those who are in his presence kneel on the ground and strike palm leaves with their hands as a sign of appreciation of his excellence. The capital of Palmares is fortified with parapets. There are keepers of the law. Although these barbarians have all but forgotten the Church they still have a chapel and images to which they direct their worship. There are other towns in charge of which are major chiefs. The second city in importance is called Subupuira and is ruled by the king's brother. It has 800 houses. It is here that Negroes are trained to fight our assaults and weapons are forged there.
>
> (Quoted in R.K. Kent, "Palmares: An African State in Brazil," *Journal of African History VI*, 2, 1965, p. 168)

In 1831 a slave named Nat Turner was inspired by what he had read in the Old Testament to lead a slave revolt in Southampton County, Virginia. At his subsequent trial he said:

> I heard a loud noise in the heavens and the Spirit instantly appeared to me and said that I should fight against the serpent [the Whites] ...
>
> I took my station in the rear and, as it was my object to carry terror and devastation wherever we went, I placed fifteen or twenty of the best armed and most to be relied on in front, who generally approached the houses as fast as their horses could run. This was for two purposes – to prevent their escape, and strike terror into the inhabitants.
>
> (Quoted in Lerone Bennett, *Pioneers in Protest*, Penguin Books Inc., 1969, pp. 91 and 95)

A few Whites were killed in the insurrection. Whites panicked and, although the revolt was soon crushed, many innocent Blacks were killed in the repression that followed. Turner fled but was caught, tried and hanged in a town called Jerusalem.

Nat Turner planning the slave revolt of 1831.

Slave owners constantly feared slave revolts. Harsh punishments were inflicted on runaways, but slaves who attacked or killed Whites or rose in revolt were invariably put to death in most brutal ways. The earliest slave revolt occurred in Hispaniola in 1522. Most slave-holding areas of America experienced insurrections. These were usually violent affairs which did not last long because the slaves lacked effective leadership. Sometimes slaves plotted revolts; at times a small incident could provoke an individual act of violence which then developed into a general

A famous biography of Toussaint L'Ouverture is *The Black Jacobins* by C.L.R. James, written nearly 50 years ago. James is a great supporter of Black rights and this is strongly expressed in his history of Haiti under Toussaint, whose achievements he describes as follows:

> **Toussaint erected fine buildings in Le Cap and built a huge monument to commemorate the abolition of slavery.**
> **Personal industry, social morality, public education, religious toleration, free trade, civic pride, racial equality, this ex-slave strove according to his lights to lay their foundations in the new State. In all his proclamations, laws and decrees he insisted on moral principles, the necessity for work, respect for law and order, pride in San Domingo, veneration for France. He sought to lift the people to some understanding of the duties and responsiblities of freedom and citizenship. It was the propaganda of a dictatorship, but not for base personal ends or the narrow interests of one class oppressing another. His government, like the absolute monarchy in its progressive days, balanced between the classes, but his was rooted in the preservation of the interests of the labouring poor . . . for the period his form of government was the best.**

A nineteenth-century engraving of Toussaint L'Ouverture.

outburst of Black hatred towards Whites and the destruction of their property. Revolts were more common in colonies, such as Jamaica, where Blacks greatly outnumbered Whites. Newly imported slaves who had been born free, and those brought from that part of West Africa that is now Ghana, were prominent in leading revolts. But slave revolts very rarely succeeded. In February 1763 a slave named Coffey led a rebellion in Berbice, Guyana. The slaves killed two-thirds of the White population of 350 and held control of the colony for a brief period before surrendering to Dutch and British troops. A large revolt in Jamaica in 1831 involving 20,000 slaves was crushed with great ferocity by the British authorities.

The only successful slave revolt was on the French-owned island of St Domingue, modern Haiti, in 1791. The sugar-rich colony had a population of nearly half a million slaves, 24,000 free people of colour (*mulattos*), and 30,000 Whites. Racial lines in Haiti were firmly drawn and rigidly upheld. "Free" coloureds bitterly resented their inferior position and wanted equality with the Whites. Many *mulattos* owned property, including slaves, and therefore, like the Whites, had an interest in preserving slavery. The ideas of the French Revolution in 1789 encouraged Whites in Haiti to think of autonomy from France while *mulattos* hoped for equality. Black slaves merely hoped for freedom from an oppressive and cruel system. In August 1791 the slaves in the north of the island rose in revolt killing Whites and destroying plantations. War had also broken out between Whites and *mulattos* and some Whites had armed their slaves. In 1793 Britain and revolutionary France went to war with each other and the National Assembly in Paris declared that all French slaves were free. One result of this was to infect other islands in the Caribbean with ideas of revolt. The British attempted to seize Haiti from the French. It was a disastrous war and thousands of British soldiers died, mainly from fever.

Among the French revolutionary forces was a freed slave, Toussaint L'Ouverture. He was a remarkable leader and took control of the forces in Haiti. He first defeated the Spanish and then the British. His aim was to make Haiti into a free but autonomous part of France. The French under the Napoleonic regime had other ideas; they wanted to reconquer Haiti and control the wealthy sugar

Slavery continued in Cuba until the 1880s. Many Black slaves escaped to join the Cuban guerilla armies fighting against the Spanish colonial rulers of the island. Esteban Montejo, in his autobiography, which was written down for him in 1963 when he was aged 104, describes escaping from the plantations:

> One day I began to keep my eye on the overseer. I had already been sizing him up for some time. That son-of-a-bitch obsessed me, and nothing could make me forget him. I think he was Spanish. I remember that he was tall and never took his hat off. All the blacks respected him because he would take the skin off your back with a single stroke of his whip. The fact is I was hot-headed that day. I don't know what came over me, but I was filled with rage which burned up just to look at the man.
>
> I whistled at him from a distance, and he looked round and then turned his back; that was when I picked up a stone and threw it at his head. I know it must have hit him because he shouted to the others to seize me. But that was the last he saw of me, because I took to the forest there and then.
>
> (Esteban Montejo, *The Autobiography of a Runaway Slave*, 1966; Penguin edition 1970, p. 36)

industry. Toussaint was tricked and captured by the French and shipped to France, where he died in prison in 1803. Back in Haiti the French army was also defeated by fever and a Black army. In 1804 Haiti was declared an Empire. Emperor Christophe, who reigned from 1806-20, attempted to rebuild the ruined economy of the island, but with little success. Haiti became the first Black independent state in the Americas, but today it has a very weak economy and is desperately poor.

9 The End of the Slave Trade and Slavery

For hundreds of years most people accepted without question the system of slavery and the trade in human beings. During the late eighteenth and early nineteenth centuries, however, in both Europe and North America the attitudes of many people slowly began to change. Increasingly, Africans were regarded as fellow human beings. There was a growing demand for the abolition of the brutal slave trade and also that slaves should be set free, or emancipated. Abolition, but particularly emancipation, involved a long and bitter political struggle in Europe and America.

The first great battle was to end the transatlantic slave trade organized by Europeans and Americans. By the late eighteenth century new political and economic ideas were being discussed about human rights and political freedom. The American Revolution of the 1770s had proclaimed that "all men are created equal" and had "inalienable rights" to "Life, Liberty and the Pursuit of Happiness", and even if that was not thought to apply to slaves it nevertheless raised some awkward questions. In France the revolution of 1789 not only promoted short-lived

An eighteenth-century engraving of the seal of the Committee for the Abolition of the Slave Trade, formed in Britain in 1787.

In the late eighteenth century there was growing opposition to the slave trade. People denounced it for humanitarian and economic reasons. The French thinker Marquis de Condorcet wrote *Reflections on Negro Slavery* in 1788.

> My friends: although I am not of your colour, I have always regarded you as my brothers. Nature has endowed you with the same mind, the same reason, the same virtues as the whites . . .; I know how often your loyalty, your honesty, your courage have made your masters blush. If one wished to find a man in the isles of America, it would not be among the people of white skin that one would find him.

Adam Smith, the Scottish economist, in his book *The Wealth of Nations* published in 1776, argued that Britain's trade and industry needed to be free of restrictions and out-dated practices.

> The experience of all ages and nations, I believe, demonstrates that the work done by slaves, though it appears to cost only their maintenance, is in the end the dearest of any. A person who can acquire no property, can have no other interest but to eat as much, and to labour as little as possible. Whatever work he does beyond what is sufficient to purchase his own maintenance can be squeezed out of him by violence only . . .

46

Granville Sharp

Granville Sharp was an active opponent of the slave trade and became chairman of the Abolition Committee. He first became involved in the slavery question in London in 1765 when he and his brother helped a young slave, Jonathan Strong, who had been savagely beaten by his master. Sharp took Strong's case to the courts and eventually won a ruling that Blacks could not be brought into England and kept as slaves.

John Calhoun (1782-1850), a southern slave-holder and politician, believed that slavery was a "good" institution.

> We of the South will not, cannot surrender our institutions. To maintain the existing relations between the two races . . . is indispensable to the peace and happiness of both. Slaveholding I hold to be a good. Never before has the black race of Africa attained a condition so civilised and so improved, not only physically, but morally and intellectually. It came here among us in a low, degraded, and savage condition, and in the course of a few generations it has grown up under the fostering care of our institutions . . . to its present civilised condition. I hold that in the present state of civilisation, where two races of different origin, and distinguished by colour, and other physical differences, as well as intellectual, are brought together, the relation now existing in the slave-holding States between the two, is, instead of an evil, a good – a positive good.

ideals about liberty which were welcomed by democrats in Britain and America but the revolutionaries freed the slaves in the French overseas colonies.

A major lead in the abolition of the slave trade was taken by Britain, which had the largest share of the trade. Starting in the 1760s the demand to end the slave trade grew into a major political pressure group. Christian and humanitarian ideas had an important influence on people's attitudes. But perhaps of equal importance was the steady change in Britain's economy away from predominantly agricultural to industrial production. The pattern and direction of British overseas trade was also changing. Britain had lost most of her North American colonies in 1783 and the West Indian sugar-producing islands steadily declined in importance as Britain expanded her trade with Asia. Many merchants supported the ideas of free trade and regarded slave labour as an inefficient way of production. Despite efforts by the West Indian lobby, which argued that Britain's economic interests rested upon a continuation of the slave trade, the British Parliament ended the slave trade in 1807. Other countries also abolished the trade – Denmark in 1802, the United States in 1808, the Netherlands in 1814, and France in 1815.

There is still considerable debate about whether or not the economies of the sugar-producing Caribbean islands were in decline when the slave trade was abolished. In many of the islands the slave population was composed of more men than women, which affected the birth rate. With the end of slave imports the labour force began to decline. Slave owners responded in two different ways. Some owners improved slave conditions in order to increase output; others, perhaps the majority, forced their slaves to work harder under harsher conditions. This led to further slave revolts in the Caribbean, such as

Emancipation of slaves in the British Caribbean, 1834. This illustration comes from a nineteenth-century history text book used in British classrooms.

Abolitionist propaganda exploited the cruelties of the slave trade. Their opponents presented a picture of happy slaves rescued from "savage Africa". In this abolitionist drawing Captain Kimber is punishing a 15-year-old slave girl for refusing his sexual advances.

THE LIBERATOR.

VOL. I.]   WILLIAM LLOYD GARRISON AND ISAAC KNAPP, PUBLISHERS.   **[NO. 22.**

BOSTON, MASSACHUSETTS.]   OUR COUNTRY IS THE WORLD—OUR COUNTRYMEN ARE MANKIND.   [SATURDAY, MAY 28, 1831.

The Liberator, the anti-slavery newspaper founded by William Lloyd Garrison in the United States in 1831. Anti-slavery sentiment was strongest in the northern states of the U.S.A. The North was more industrial than the Southern States, which continued to rely on slave labour for agricultural production until emancipation in the 1860s.

Commodore Sir Charles Hotham reporting to the British Admiralty on the destruction of slave factories at Gallinas, West Africa, 13 February 1849:

On the 3rd I assembled my seven ships off Gallinas, and with a force of 300 men landed at Dombocorro, took possession of it, and the neighbouring factories and barracoons [slave pens], and planted sentinels to guard the property. In the meantime, Captain Jones pushed on to the Solyman factories which, along with the village of Dreesing, known for its intimate connection with the slave trade, he totally destroyed. On the following morning the large factories in the vicinity of Domboocorro were, with the goods which they contained, entirely destroyed; and at 1 pm on the same day, Domboocorro itself, with all its contents was burnt to the ground.

(*Parliamentary Papers*, 1850, IX, 53, p. 460)

---

the revolts of 1823 and 1831. It also raised opposition to slavery in Britain, which by the mid-1820s had become a popular political cause. Large meetings were held throughout the country and in the 1830s a further Act of Parliament brought slavery to an end in the British Empire. Many slave owners feared violence from freed slaves. In fact, the emancipation which ended several hundred years of slavery passed off peacefully.

France ended slavery in her colonies in 1848 but in many parts of America the system continued for several more decades. In the United States slaves were mainly confined to the agricultural states of the south. Expanding trade, and especially technological changes in cotton processing and an increased demand for cotton clothing, meant that the southern states continued to require cheap slave labour for the plantations. Unlike the British colonies of the Caribbean the U.S. slave population was fairly well balanced and fertile and thus able to increase rapidly in size from 1.2 million in 1810 to 4 million in 1860. As a result, slavery continued in the United States for 30 years after the British had emancipated their slaves. Many Americans opposed it, particularly in the northern states of the Union. The American Anti-Slavery Society, founded in 1833, led a great moral crusade against slavery which divided the country. The issue of slavery was one of the causes of the bitter civil war that was fought between the North and the South between 1861 and 1865. At the end of the war the proclamation of emancipation freed the slaves.

Cuba and Brazil were not able to meet the continuing demand for cheap slave labour for the sugar, coffee and tobacco plantations. Both countries continued to import slaves from Africa throughout the first half of the nineteenth century. It is estimated that two million slaves were brought across the Atlantic in the years 1811-70, the majority going to Brazil.

Britain provided the lead in the international attempts to stop this "illegitimate" trade of people

The temporary court house at Morant Bay, Jamaica where the "rebels" of the 1865 "revolt" were tried. Soldiers can be seen guarding the accused.

from Africa. Various means were used: treaties were signed to restrict Spanish and Portuguese and Brazilian slave trading; slavers in Africa were attacked by gunboats and their *barracoons* destroyed; and slave ships were seized by British men-o-war and their cargoes landed at ports such as Freetown and Libreville in West Africa. African traders were encouraged to sell "legitimate" trade goods such as palm oil and groundnuts, which were increasingly in demand by the industries of Europe, in place of slaves. Nevertheless, the illegal trade in slaves continued until the 1860s, the Brazilians and Cubans being the main culprits. Emancipation of slaves in those countries came in the late 1880s as a result of new attitudes, wars involving Black soldiers and changing economic and political conditions.

The end of slavery had little immediate impact on the way of life of most Blacks in America. Slaves might be legally free but most remained poor, without land and easily exploited for their labour. Strong tensions existed in many areas between the White ruling classes and free Blacks and former slaves. In Jamaica a small number of Blacks became prosperous merchants and independent farmers. Their new status and their influence over other Blacks were resented by the White plantocracy who looked for opportunities to exclude them from any share in the government of the island. In eastern Jamaica in 1865 economic hardships led to increased tension between Blacks and the White authorities. The Whites may have feared a Black rebellion like that of Haiti 70 years before. A minor court case and riot at Morant Bay was used by the British governor as an excuse to deal with Black demands. Troops were called out and the

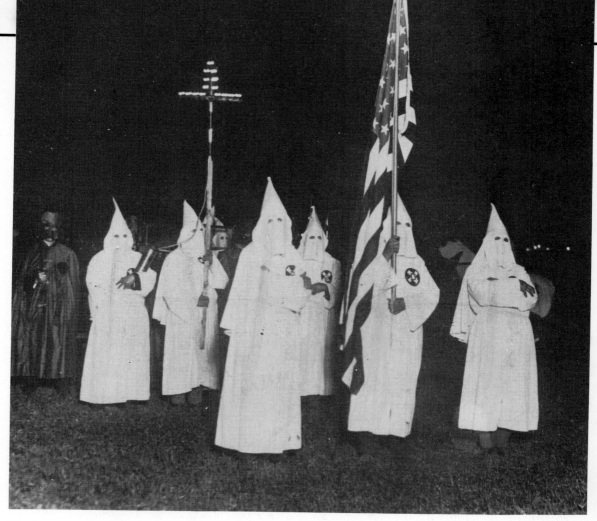

The Ku Klux Klan was at its most powerful in the late nineteenth and early twentieth centuries. To disguise themselves, and also to frighten Black people, the Klansmen put on white robes and hoods.

supposed "rebellion" brutally put down and hundreds of Blacks killed. The British Government responded by getting rid of the governor and taking over direct control of the government of Jamaica.

After emancipation in the United States in 1865 Blacks were encouraged to help in the "reconstruction" of the war-damaged South. All the time that federal troops remained in the southern states the Blacks received some protection.

By a Civil Rights Act of 1866 all Blacks were granted U.S. citizenship, a right reinforced by the Fourteenth Amendment to the U.S. Constitution two years later. However, laws did not change White attitudes. Most Blacks were poor and in the rural areas many former slaves became sharecroppers, working White-owned land in return for a small share of the proceeds from the sale of the crop. Blacks registered to vote in state elections and in South Carolina they briefly controlled the state legislature. With the withdrawal of federal troops local Whites prevented Blacks from voting and excluded them from the public schools. A White terrorist organization called the Ku Klux Klan intimidated and murdered Blacks who tried to claim their civil rights. Social, political and economic discrimination against Blacks kept them in inferior positions, not only in the southern states but throughout the whole of the United States for more than a hundred years after the ending of slavery.

10 Afro-Americans in America, Europe and Africa

This book has been about the forced movement and settlement of Blacks from Africa to the American continent over the period 1520-1870. As a result of this brutal business all the countries in America from Argentina and Chile in the south to Canada in the north have populations which include Black people, or Afro-Americans. Today, the largest Afro-American populations are in those areas which received most slaves – the coastlands of Brazil, the islands of the Caribbean, and the southern and eastern states of the United States.

Poverty and political and economic oppression have encouraged Blacks to move to new areas. After the U.S. civil war Black slaves became free but even in states where they formed the majority they were easily discriminated against and treated as inferiors by the Whites. Many Blacks in the rural southern states were also unemployed. To escape these conditions thousands of Blacks moved north to the industrial cities such as New York, Chicago, Philadelphia and Baltimore. Afro-Americans in Brazil also moved into the cities and the interior of the vast country. In the predominantly Afro-American islands of the Caribbean early in the twentieth century some Blacks found work on the mainland of central America building the Panama Canal (opened 1914) and on fruit plantations. Other Blacks emigrated to North America where they hoped to find a better life.

A small trickle of Blacks from the Caribbean came to Europe in the eighteenth, nineteenth and early twentieth centuries. This book opened with an account of the life of Olaudah Equiano who was a Black immigrant to Britain in the mid-eighteenth century. When he settled in London there may have been as many as 15,000 people of African origin in the country. Most lived in major ports, specially those connected with the slave trade, such as London, Bristol and Liverpool. Small Black communities also grew up in other ports – Cardiff's Tiger Bay area for example. But Black people could be found all over Britain. They had come as seamen, soldiers, and labourers or been brought in as servants and slaves. The total number of Blacks in Britain in the mid-eighteenth century was roughly in the same proportion as the Black population of Britain in 1960.

Throughout the nineteenth and early twentieth centuries a small number of Afro-Americans came to Britain to study at university. Some

A Black Professional in Britain
John and Caroline Barbour-James, London, c. 1912. John Barbour-James was born in British Guiana in 1867. He worked in the civil service there and also in the British West African colony of the Gold Coast. He settled in Britain before the First World War and lived in Acton, London.

Officially, Blacks were not accepted into the British army during the First World War until late 1918. Nevertheless some recruiting officers accepted Black Britons and Blacks from overseas who had come to Europe to enlist. John Williams joined up at the age of 20. He fought in France, was wounded four times, and gained several medals including the Military Medal and the French Legion of Honour.

John Williams, featured in an article in the African Telegraph and Gold Coast Mirror *in March 1919.*

returned home but many stayed to work as doctors, dentists, musicians, clergymen and at other professional jobs. During the First and Second World Wars Blacks also came to Britain to join the armed forces or to do war work in the factories and as foresters.

The largest movement of Blacks from the Caribbean to settle in Britain came after the Second World War. All the British colonies in the Caribbean were relatively poor; the economies of the islands depended on a few export crops such as sugar and there was very little industry. Unemployment and underemployment were very high. At the same time, Britain was desperately short of workers to help rebuild her war-damaged economy. Thousands of people from the Caribbean islands came to Britain to work. At first life for many of these new immigrants was very difficult. The surroundings were strange, the weather was cold, and it was not easy to find somewhere to live. White people often acted very rudely and all too frequently Blacks were forced to take the kind of jobs that most White people did not want to do. Britain might have been a strange and often hostile place for Black immigrants, but it also offered work and a chance to make a new life. Blacks settled down, bought homes, and raised families. A similar process also happened in France and the Netherlands as Black people came from French and Dutch colonies in the Caribbean to live and work in Europe.

Back to Africa

Ever since the transatlantic slave trade began Blacks who were taken to America thought of going back to Africa. Some runaway slaves hoped to find a way of returning "home", or created an African-like way of life in their hideaways in the forests and inaccessible areas of America. Small groups of "free" Blacks in America and Britain planned to establish settlements on the coast of West Africa. The first of these was Freetown, set up in 1787 by a committee of British Black and White humanitarians, including Olaudah Equiano. It was intended as a settlement for poor Blacks from Britain, and also for Black "loyalists" who had fought on the side of the British during the American War of Independence and who had been resettled in Nova Scotia in Canada. After the abolition of the slave trade in 1807 the population of Freetown grew as the cargoes rescued from slave ships were landed there.

In the United States the "Back to Africa" movement was seen by Blacks to have two main purposes: first, it would enable Black people to escape from White domination and create new Black societies; and, secondly, the Black settlers would introduce into Africa modern ideas of Christianity and "civilization". The settlements along the coast of what is now Liberia were organized into an independent Black republic in 1847. The Black settlers in West Africa were few in number. They fought wars of conquest against the African peoples and ran the country largely in their own interests.

Marcus Garvey.

Marcus Garvey (1887-1940)

Marcus Garvey was a Jamaican who believed that Blacks in America should take a pride in their colour. He went to the United States and founded the Universal Negro Improvement Association, which demanded "Africa for the Africans, at home and abroad". The real solution for Black people in America, he argued, was to "return home" to Africa. Garvey founded the Black Star Steamship Line to transport emigrants to Africa. Although he had a large following in the U.S.A. very few Blacks wished to go to Africa. In 1920, when he was at the height of his popularity, Garvey declared

himself provisional President of the African Republic. He told a mass meeting in New York:

> The Negroes of the world say, "We are striking homewards towards Africa to make the big black republic." And in the making of Africa a big Black republic, what is the barrier? The barrier is the White man; and we say to the White man who now dominates Africa that it is to his interest to clear out of Africa now, because . . . we are coming 400,000,000 strong, and we mean to retake every square inch of the twelve million square miles of African territory belonging to us by right Divine. . . . We are out to get what has belonged to us politically, economically, and in every way.

The UNIA collapsed and Garvey was accused of fraud and imprisoned. Although Garvey died poor and virtually forgotten in London his movement inspired many Blacks in both America and colonial Africa to demand civil rights and national independence.

The Rastafarians

The Rastafarian movement, or way of life, began in Jamaica in the 1930s. It drew inspiration from the Bible and also from Marcus Garvey's belief that a Black king would be crowned in Africa as a sign of Black deliverance. When Ras Tafari was crowned Emperor of Ethiopia in 1930 many poor and landless Blacks in Jamaica saw this as the expected sign. Rastafarians, or Rasta as they like to be known, believe themselves to be the true Jews. They reject "White" culture, uphold divine healing and folk medicine, and smoke or drink the drug *ganga*, or Indian hemp, as sacramental medicine. Only a handful of Rastas have gone to live in Africa and very few African governments encouraged them to do so.

Civil Rights in the United States

Afro-Americans form 10 per cent of the population of the United States. For many years in the twentieth century Blacks suffered from social, economic and political discrimination. Compared to Whites the Black population had a higher infant mortality rate, spent fewer years at secondary school, had lower paid jobs, found it difficult to get into the professions, had poorer housing, owned fewer cars and consumer goods, suffered from

Airmen from the Caribbean who came to Britain during the Second World War (1939-45) to help in the struggle against the fascist powers.

Black immigrants arriving in Britain to look for work in the late 1940s.

more diseases, and died at a younger age. In many states of the Union Blacks were prevented from voting and were treated as inferiors. Some Black intellectuals believed that Afro-Americans should work hard to prove that they were as good as Whites and also organize themselves to gain civil rights. They did not like the separatist ideas of Garvey and the "Back to Africa" movement, which they regarded as unreal fantasies. Their view was that Blacks had helped to make the United States rich and powerful and they should, therefore, claim their share of that wealth and power. The National Association for the Advancement of Colored People (NAACP) was formed in 1910 chiefly to fight against racial discrimination and lynching. The National Urban League, set up in 1911, helped Blacks who moved in thousands to the big cities of the north to adjust to their new environment and find jobs. Black trade unions attempted to get fairer treatment for Black workers, but there were serious race riots, especially during the First and Second World Wars, in northern cities such as East St Louis (1917) and Detroit (1943).

The great economic boom in the United States in the 1950s and 1960s brought a break-through in racial civil rights. The United States Supreme Court declared that racially segregated public schools were illegal, although Federal troops had to be used to enforce the law in certain southern states. Throughout the South Whites tried to prevent the desegregation of schools and public amenities. In December 1955 a Black woman in Montgomery, Alabama, Mrs Rosa Parks, refused

Mrs Gene Martin, a midwife, came to Britain from Jamaica in 1960. Her husband Francis arrived in 1958; in Jamaica he was a smallholder and helped to run a small pentecostal church. In Britain he became a metal worker. Mrs Martin's first job in Britain was as a ward orderly in a Fulham hospital. She now works at the Pepperpot Club in London, a day centre for Afro-Caribbean people. On 15 April 1986 she gave an interview to the *Guardian* newspaper:

It was our desire to return home before the five years on our passports were up. But we got so used to living here and things had changed so much there. There were plenty of jobs to begin with, even though wages were small, five pounds and six pence a week. You put up with the strange food, the rain, cramped living – and managing without the children.

[Four of Mr & Mrs Martin's five children were born in Jamaica]. My husband's mother was looking after them until 1968. There was no savings at all. There was one person's money to keep us; and the other person's to keep the children.

When I came over, my husband lived in Faraday Road (North Kensington). He was a tenant; his sister had the house. It was cramped. Honestly, I couldn't get used to it. There was the bed, there was the cooker, there was the pail, there was the food cupboard – all in one room. You were able to get accommodation at that time, though it was only one room. The only time it began to get bad was when they put up notices – No Irish, No Coloureds.

to move out of a "Whites only" seat on a bus. This started a whole new stage in the civil rights movement. Blacks used passive resistance. Dr Martin Luther King, a Black Baptist minister, preached non-violent opposition and organized the Southern Christian Leadership Conference. Radical students, both Black and White, who helped lead the struggle against discrimination faced police and mob violence, and murder. In 1963 a huge march on Washington by 250,000 people demanded full civil rights for Blacks. When the U.S. Government was slow to pass laws to help protect and advance the Black community some Blacks turned to violence. Eventually a Civil Rights Act was passed in 1964, followed by a Voting Rights Act in 1965. Despite new laws and great social and economic advances made by Afro-Americans in the United States since the 1960s many Blacks still remain among the poorest sector of the population in the richest country in the world.

I stand in the middle of two opposing forces in the Negro community. One is the force of complacency made up of Negroes who have been so completely drained of self-respect that they have adjusted to segregation and those Negroes who profit by segregation. The other force is one of bitterness and hatred. . . . It is expressed in the various black nationalist groups, the largest and best known being Elijah Muhammad's Muslim Movement. This movement is nourished by the frustration over the continued existence of racial discrimination. I have tried to stand between these two forces saying there is a more excellent way of love and non-violent protest. If this philosophy had not emerged I am convinced that by now many streets of the South would be flowing with floods of blood.

The Revd. Martin Luther King was murdered in Memphis, Tennessee, in April 1968. He had gone to the city to support a strike of Black sanitation workers.

Street scenes in Harlem, the Black quarter in New York, in the 1930s.

Roger Bastide, a French anthropologist, describes part of a Yoruba religious ritual in Brazil:

Early in the morning animal sacrifices take place: two-footed beasts for *Eshú*, four-footed ones for the principal deity whose day it is. Next comes the preparation for the feast, especially for cooking of those dishes that will be offered to the gods who are being invoked. Towards evening comes the *padé de Eshú*, which opens the dancing, and involves an invocation to the god who intermediates between human beings and the *orisha*. This is immediately followed by the "summons" to all the known *orisha*, beat out on the three drums, its rhythms varying according to the god who is being

addressed. Each one is also honoured by the performance of three "hymns" in the Yoruba language. During the course of the dances which accompany these musical offerings, the *orisha* descend on their children, who pass into a tranced state and are carried inside the sanctuary. After a short break the singing and dancing are resumed, exclusively by those initiates who have undergone possession, and who have now reassumed their liturgical vestments. Finally, the gods are expelled (i.e. the trances are brought to an end) by a series of "hymns" performed in the reverse order to that which accompanied their summoning.

(Roger Bastide, *African Civilisations in the New World*, C. Hurst, 1971, p. 119)

A Black jazz band in the United States, 1919.

Black Cultural Diffusion

Very often African slaves were stripped naked before being loaded on board ship for the voyage across the Atlantic to the Americas. But Africans brought with them their languages, and their ideas and practices about religion, music, warfare, medicine, history and family life. These aspects of African culture were introduced into America and then adapted in a variety of ways. African language structures, idioms and words exist among rural Black communities in Brazil, the Caribbean, and the southern states of the United States. Folk tales about Anansi, the spider man, are told in both West Africa and in Jamaica. Many religious beliefs and practices clearly show a direct African influence. For example, ideas about the Yoruba storm god, Shango, were taken to Brazil and elsewhere in America, as was belief in *vudu*, the word for "god" among the Fon of Dahomey, which appears as voodoo in Haiti. Besides these preserved religions other religious ideas have also been merged into Roman Catholic and Protestant Christianity. One major African influence that has gone beyond the Afro-American communities in the Americas is music and dance. Blues, jazz, calypso, steel bands, and reggae are all part of the rich musical contribution that Africa has made to the world via the transatlantic slave trade.

Glossary

abolition the movement to end the slave trade.

Americas the lands of the American continent, including North, Central and South America and the islands of the Caribbean.

assegay, or assegai a short stabbing spear.

barracoon a fenced enclosure or building in which slaves were imprisoned.

bondservant a slave, or a servant with very limited freedom.

coffle a column, or caravan, of slaves chained together.

Conquistadores the Spanish conquerors of Central and South America.

diaspora dispersion, or scattering, of people.

emancipation the liberation of slaves; the Emancipation movement campaigned to end slavery.

factor the agent of a trading company on the coast of West Africa; the forts and trading houses were sometimes known as *factories*.

fort a defended warehouse or trading centre on the west coast of Africa.

hadith the traditions; the sayings of the Muslim prophet Muhammad.

husbandry farming or agricultural work.

indentured labourer a person who is bound by a legal agreement to work for a set number of years, e.g. an apprentice.

Islam to submit to the will of God. See *Muslim* below.

middleman in trade a person who buys from one source and then sells to another.

middle passage the sea journey across the Atlantic Ocean from Africa to the Americas.

Muslim a follower of the religion of Islam.

panyarring kidnapping people to be sold as slaves.

pawn a person who is enslaved because he or she has fallen into debt.

plantation an agricultural estate worked by slaves or other kinds of labour who live on the estate.

plantocracy the powerful planters in the Caribbean islands and the southern states of the United States.

Quaker a member of the Religious Society of Friends.

Qur'an the book of the revelations to Muhammad; the holy book of Muslims.

seasoning the process of breaking in, or accustoming, slaves to the work on the plantation.

sharecropper a tenant farmer who pays the rent from part of the crop that is grown.

slave economy where slave labour produces most of the wealth of an economy.

slaver someone involved in buying and selling slaves; also a slave ship.

Sudan the region of Africa between the Red Sea and the Atlantic Ocean. The western Sudan is the area in the interior of West Africa south of the Sahara Desert.

voodoo religious practices largely consisting of spirit worship.

West India Lobby the wealthy planters in the British Caribbean islands who tried to influence the Government in London.

Date List

1415	Portuguese capture Ceuta in north Africa.
1440s	First slaves brought by sea from West Africa to Europe.
1481	Trading fort at Elmina, Gold Coast, built by Portuguese.
1490	King of Kongo invites Portuguese to send missionaries and craftsmen to his country.
1492	Columbus sails across the Atlantic and reaches America.
1513	First African slaves imported into America.
1530	Sugar production begins in Brazil.
1619	Black slaves first introduced into English colonies of North America.
1620s	English settlements begin on West Indian islands; start of sugar production and export to Europe.
1630-45	Dutch control over sugar-producing region of north-east Brazil.
1655	English capture Jamaica from Spaniards; great increase in slave imports for the English plantations.
1700s	Great increase in the transatlantic slave trade; Britain dominates the trade.
1756	Olaudah Equiano taken to the West Indies as a slave.
1783	United States becomes independent of Great Britain.
1787	Settlement of "poor Blacks" at Freetown, Sierra Leone, on the west coast of Africa.
1791	Successful slave revolt in West Indian island of St Domingue (Haiti) led by Toussaint L'Ouverture.
1808	Britain and the United States declare the international slave trade to be illegal for their citizens.
1822	Afro-Americans who have returned to West Africa establish the settlement of Liberia.
1831	Nat Turner leads a slave revolt in Virginia, United States.
1834	Abolition of slavery in the British Empire.
1847	Liberia becomes an independent republic.
1861-5	Civil war in the United States which leads to the end of slavery.
1880	End of slavery in Spanish West Indian island of Cuba.
1888	Slavery abolished in Brazil.
1910	National Association for the Advancement of Colored People founded in the United States.
1914-18	First World War.
1920	Universal Negro Improvement Association led by Marcus Garvey at its height in the United States.
1930	Rastafarian movement begins in Jamaica.
1939-45	Second World War.
1950s	Immigrants from the West Indian islands come to Britain, France, and the Netherlands in increasing numbers in search of work.
1957	Gold Coast becomes the independent state of Ghana.
1962	Jamaica becomes independent from Britain.
1960s	Struggle for Black civil rights in the United States.
1968	Murder of Martin Luther King in Memphis, Tennessee.

Book List

Roger Anstey, *The Atlantic Slave Trade and British Abolition, 1760-1810*, Macmillan, 1975

*William Claypole and John Robottom, *Caribbean Story*, 2 vols, Longman, 1981

Philip Curtin, *The Atlantic Slave Trade. A Census*, Wisconsin University Press, 1969

*Paul Edwards (ed.), *Equiano's Story*, Heinemann 1967

*Nigel File and Chris Power, *Black Settlers in Britain 1555-1958*, Heinemann, 1981

John Hope Franklin, *From Slavery to Freedom A History of the American Negro*, 1947; and subsequent editions

Peter Fryer, *Staying Power. A History of Black People in Britain*, Pluto, 1984

E.D. Genovese, *Roll, Jordan, Roll*, Deutsch, 1975

P.E.H. Hair, *The Atlantic Slave Trade and Black Africa*, Historical Association pamphlet No. 93, 1978

J.E. Inikori (ed.), *Forced Migration. The Impact of the Export Slave Trade on African Societies*, Hutchinson, 1982

C.L.R. James, *The Black Jacobins. Toussaint L'Ouverture and the San Domingo Revolution*, 1938;

Allison & Busby, 1980

Winthrop D. Jordan, *White over Black. American Attitudes toward the Negro, 1550-1812*, Penguin Books, Baltimore U.S.A., 1969

*David Killingray, *The Slave Trade*, Harrap, 1974

Paul Lovejoy, *Transformations in Slavery*, Cambridge, 1983

Edward Reynolds, *Stand the Storm. A History of the Atlantic Slave Trade*, Allison and Busby, 1985

Leslie B. Rout Jr., *The African Experience in Spanish America*, Cambridge, 1976

P.M. Sherlock, *West Indian Nations. A New History*, Macmillan, 1973

James Walvin, *The Negro and English Society, 1555-1945*, Allen Lane, 1975

James Walvin, *Slavery and the Slave Trade. A Short Illustrated History*, Macmillan, 1983

John White and Ralph Willett, *Slavery in the American South*, Longman, 1973

* indicates a book suitable for younger secondary school students

Acknowledgments

The Author and Publishers would like to thank the following for permission to reproduce illustrations: BBC Hulton Picture Library for pages 51, 54 and 55 (bottom); Bristol City Library for page 31; The British Library for page 53; The British Museum for page 8; Mary Evans Picture Library for pages 26, 30, 48 (top), 49, 50 and 58; Jeffrey P. Green for page 52; The *Guardian* for page 56; Imperial War Museum for page 55 (top); Longman Group Ltd for the map on page 40 (taken from *Caribbean Story, Book I*, by William Claypole and John Robottom); Mansell Collection for pages 42 and 57 (top and bottom); The *Observer* for page 41; Iris Orego for page 14 (from *The Merchant of Prato*, published by Jonathan Cape Ltd); Royal Commonwealth Society for pages 6, 16, 17 (top), 38 and 39 (top and bottom); Wilberforce Museum, Hull for the frontispiece and pages 24 (right and left), 28, 33 (bottom), 46, 47 and 48 (bottom). Illustrations on pages 11, 17 (bottom), 21, 27, 35, 36 and 37 are from the Author's own collection. The map on page 7 was drawn by R.F. Brien. The graph on page 33 is based on a graph in Philip D. Curtin, *The Atlantic Slave Trade; A Census*, Wisconsin University Press, 1969.

Cover Illustrations

The colour print shows slaves being branded, from "A Scene on the Coast of Africa" by Biard (*Wilberforce Museum, Hull*); the black and white print shows a street scene in Harlem in the 1930s (*Mansell Collection*); the figure of the slave was drawn by Nick Theato.

Index